BIKE Lanarkshire
the Lowther Hills and the Clyde valley
25 road and off-road cycle tours

Paul Lamarra

Tinto Press

Copyright Tinto Press, 2007

Published by Tinto Press, c/o Rural Development Trust, 1 Powell Street, Douglas Water, ML11 9PP

British Library Cataloguing in Publication Data
A CIP record for this book is available from the British Library.

ISBN: 978 – 0954228521

Typesetting & design by Iwik Designs

Cover Design: Iwik Designs

Photographs: Paul Lamarra

Cover Photographs: top right - Leadhills; top left – Nutberry Hill; bottom – ford, Candy Mill.

Maps: Michelle Thomson – South Lanarkshire Council

Printed by: CCB Print, Glasgow

For Iain

SOUTH
LANARKSHIRE
RURAL
PARTNERSHIP

Acknowledgements

I would like to thank the following for their generous assistance: Hugh Murray, Chris Parkin, Gordon Muir, Carmichael estates, Yvonne Rogers, Michelle Thomson, Robyn Frew, Simon Pilpel and Alan Bannister.

Bike Lanarkshire

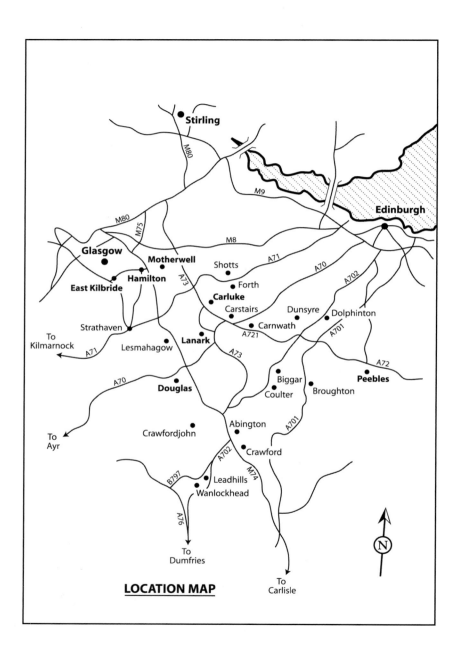

LOCATION MAP

CONTENTS

INTRODUCTION

USING THE GUIDE

Of the routes described in this book it is only on the reservoir routes and the Nutberry hill route that you will be required to re-trace your outward journey. Five of the routes involve off-road sections.

Each route is described in the direction that I have found through experience derives the greatest benefit from the prevailing winds and the terrain.

Most of the routes start from or are in the vicinity of Biggar, Lanark, Strathaven or in the Lowther hills. The routes are organised into chapters according to their starting point and a visitor guide to each town or area, detailing how to get there, where to eat and where to stay, opens each chapter.

Each route has a preamble that gives a brief description, the distance, the grade and a guide to the terrain. All of which should allow you to decide on its suitability. Following on is a list of points of interest to watch out for, some background information and refreshment stops en route.

This is followed by detailed directions with a distance indicator and an outline map. For the road routes the maps provided or the OS road map – Southern Scotland, should be sufficient. However for the off-road routes the OS Explorer or Landranger maps are best.

When the progress between two points is less than quarter of a mile the distance is omitted.

CYCLING

Preparation
It is all to easy to jump on the bike and go but a more enjoyable day out is more likely if your bike is properly maintained.

Check the bike over before you cycle. Tighten anything that is loose that shouldn't be, check the brakes and see that the chain is clean and well lubricated.

Properly inflated tyres are essential for efficient cycling and consider using smooth tyres for road cycling and knobbly tyres only for off-road cycling. Using the gears effectively will also extend the length of the route you can comfortably manage.

What to wear? What to carry?

Specialised clothing is not necessary but you will do well to choose clothes that mimic its qualities. Shorts or trousers that are quick drying and permit easy movement are best – but they shouldn't be so loose that there is a danger of them becoming entangled.

Gloves are a good idea even on a good day as they will protect your hands in a fall and delay the onset of pressure sores. Shoes with a stiff sole will offer the most comfort.

Let the weather be your guide. In cold weather wear lots of thin layers that can be peeled away as you warm up. In summer wear clothes that let air circulate freely but it is always advisable to carry a waterproof - the brighter the better.

Opinion is divided on whether wearing a helmet should be compulsory but it is probably best to err on the side of caution and wear one anyway.

It is essential that you carry a puncture repair kit, tyre levers and one or two spare inner tubes. A lightweight multipurpose spanner and the necessary Allen keys should also be included per party. A bicycle lock is always a good idea..

Most importantly carry something to eat that will replace lost energy and plenty of water – on hot days take special care not to dehydrate.

Safety

Following this basic advice will contribute to a safe day's cycling:

Acquaint yourself with the Highway Code.

Cycle two abreast except where visibility is restricted. There is often slow farm machinery and livestock on the roads, so be ready to stop and be patient.

If it is at all possible that you will have to cycle after dark ensure that you have lights in working order fitted to your bike.

Do not overload your bike and try to use luggage specifically designed for cycling. When using panniers take care to ensure the load is balanced and put the heaviest items to the bottom.

Be aware of other road users especially pedestrians and horse riders.

Warn each other of impending hazards – for example shout "hole" and point to it.

Cycling with children

I have cycled many of the routes with my own children on-tow on trailer bike or in a child seat. Older children will be able to tackle some of the routes under their own steam. However I would suggest you avoid the section on the A70 between Carstairs and Ravenstruther of the Lanark, Tinto and Covington route and the A70 and A73 sections of the Lanark, Douglas and Roberton route.

Extra special care is required when cycling with children and it is a good idea to take measures to make them more visible – for example flags can be purchased from bike shops that can be attached to a child's bike.

It is best to allow them to cycle just inside of you but slightly ahead where you can keep an eye on them.

My children love a day out on the bikes but I have learned many hard lessons while cycling with them. Try not to attempt more than an hour at a time; have another purpose to the day that will motivate them, such as a picnic or a visit to a play park; keep a check on their comfort and as children can tire very quickly have a plan B.

Off-road cycling

Off-road cycling requires you to be very well-prepared as there is much less room for error. In addition to the usual safeguards ensure that you leave details of your route and expected time of arrival. Some sections of the off-road routes included in this book are very remote and a long walk may be necessary to find help.

The Scottish Outdoor Access Code

SCOTTISH
OUTDOOR ACCESS CODE

KNOW THE CODE BEFORE YOU GO ...
ENJOY SCOTLAND'S OUTDOORS -
RESPONSIBLY!

Everyone has the right to be on most land and inland water providing they act responsibly. Your access rights and responsibilities are explained fully in the Scottish Outdoor Access Code. Whether you're in the outdoors or managing the outdoors, the key things are to:

- take responsibility for your own actions;
- respect the interests of other people;
- care for the environment.

Find out more by visiting **www.outdooraccess-scotland.com** or phoning your local Scottish Natural Heritage office.

WHERE TO GO
People now have the right of access to most land in Scotland, including private roads, tracks and paths, for recreation and to get from place to place. This right is conditional on people acting responisbly.

The main exceptions to the new right are: people's gardens, farmyards (although access if often possible - if in doubt ask), and land in which crops have been sown or growing (but you can use the field margins as long as you avoid unnecesary damage to crops).

You can take access to golf courses (except green and tees), but only to cross the area without interfering with play - cyclists need to keep to the paths at all times.

TAKE RESPONSIBILITY FOR YOUR OWN ACTIONS
Use common sense to avoid accidents - show care and consideration and make sure speed doesn't alarm or endanger others.

The outdoors is not risk-free! Be aware of natural hazards such as clifss, loose rocks, tree roots and ice.

Follow advice on signs advising of activities such as tree felling, crop spraying or other activities/ events - you may need to alter your route.

Take extra care if you are in charge of children to ensure they enjoy the outdoors responsibly and safely.

CARE FOR THE ENVIRONMENT

Cycling on hard surfaces, such as wide paths ands tracks causes few problems. If going off-trail, especially in winter, avoid wet, boggy or soft ground and don't churn up the surface.

Take care not to disturb wildlife or damage natural vegetation; observe information or signs advising you of sensitive sites.

Take your litter away with you.

A group will have greater impact on the enviroment, so take extra care.

RESPECT THE INTERESTS OF OTHERS

Respect people's privacy by keeping a sensible distance from houses

Respect people's property, including machineray, gates and fences – leave gates as you find them

Be considerate to other users of the outdoors such as walkers and horse riders; slow down and alert them to your presence. On narow paths give way or dismount if necessary

Take care not to alarm farm animals, including stock on open ground, horses and wildlife; take extra care during lambing season

If you have a dog with you, keep it under proper control at all times

Avoid crossing land when shooting or deer stalking is taking place; find out if your planed route will be affected and seek advice on alternative routes

Keep noise levels and potential disturbance to a minimum, especially if riding at night

Keep access points clear; park your car where it won't cause problems and don't lock your bike to gates

RESPONSIBILITES OF LAND MANAGERS

Land managers also have responsibilities under the code to:

respect access rights and have people's needs for a safe and enjoyable visit.

Act reasonably when asking people to avoid land managemnet operations.

Work with your local authority and others to help intergrate access and land management.

Wanlockhead: old lead mine and beam engine.

THE LOWTHER ROUTES

Mention the Lowther Hills and most people will respond with a puzzled look. Describe them as the Leadhills and the same people will respond with a spark of recognition. Leadhills is in fact a Lowther village but it is possibly the best name for this range of hills because for the last two millennia, at least, theses hills have been mined for their minerals and especially lead.

It was with this in mind that the hills were, in the 19th century, re-christened by the Rev Moir Porteous as God's Own Treasure House in Scotland. However the treasure to be found in the Lowther Hills, and in particular gold, was not extracted for God but for Elizabeth I by Bevis Bulmer and for the Scottish crown jewels. Later it was the earl of Hopetoun and the duke of Buccleuch that benefited from the deposits of lead and zinc.

The piles of spoil, the old railway tracks, the ruined mine buildings and the extensive network of ancient paths do not detract from the bleak wildness or beauty of the Lowthers. Rather the mining detritus and the villages of Wanlockhead and Leadhills which are so redolent of the mining era, form a visible layer of human endeavour that combines with the mysterious landscape of steep cleuchs and sun-starved valleys to provides a compelling and fascinating experience.

Although the Lowther Hills are low and rounded the extensive views of rolling hills can still induce a sense of awe as can a journey that takes in the glaciated Dalveen valley or the steep-sided Mennock pass.

GETTING THERE
Leave the M74 at junction 13 and follow signs for Abington. To continue to Crawford follow the A702 south from Abington. To reach Leadhills and Wanlockhead turn right just south of Abington to follow the B797 south. From Edinburgh follow the A702 south via Biggar.

STAYING

Days Inn	M74 junction 13, Abington	01864 502782
Abington Hotel	Carlisle Road, Abington	01864 502467
Heatherghyll Motel	20 Carlisle Road, Crawford	01864 502641
Crawford Arms Hotel	111 Carlisle Road, Crawford	01864 502262
Lyndsey Towers	30 Carlisle Road, Crawford	01864 502855
Holmlands B&B	22 Carlisle Road Crawford	01864 502753
Rob Roy Caravan Park	Carlisle Road, Crawford	01524 64829
Meadowfoot Cottage	6 Gowanbank, Leadhills	01659 74369
Hopetoun Arms Hotel	37 Main Street, Leadhills	01659 7423
Lotus Lodge Youth Hostel	Wanlockhead	01659 74252

Crawfordjohn: the climb to the Apache pass.

THE LOWTHER HILL PASSES

For such a compact range of hills there are a surprising number of ancient routes and byways looking for the easiest way through the hills. This route, and the shorter alternative, connects the routes over the high passes that are still in use today.

Throughout the roads are delightfully peaceful and excellent views, which are often dramatic, are always on offer. From Drumlanrig onwards the scenery is gentler as is the cycling. Once the high ground has been achieved the cycle along the hedgerow-lined lane above the Nith, and by the Nith, is as good as cycling can get.

Big loop/Wee loop
Distance: 52 miles/33 miles
Grade: hard/moderate
Terrain: the road surfaces are on the whole excellent. The big loop is demanding and involves three significant climbs. The wee loop involves only two significant climbs.
Map: OS Road Map 3, Southern Scotland & Northumberland

By the way
CRAWFORDJOHN

Crawfordjohn occupies the only truly habitable spot between a wide expanse of moorland that stretches away to the north and the Lowther hills to the south.

An ecclesiastical site since medieval times and a burgh of barony since 1688, it was the preferred base of the Cameronians, the Covenanter regiment, after the settlement of 1690.

Colebrooke Arms   7 Main Street   01864 504 239

APACHE PASS (both loops)
Named by local cyclists the Apache pass links Crawfordjohn with Leadhills. The summit of the pass at 366 metres (104 metre ascent) is reached in just less than two miles. Once over the pass and through the trees there are extensive views over the Lowthers and the Clyde valley.

LEADHILLS (both loops)
Leadhills is still easily identified as a mining village even though it is 70 years since mining ceased. A factory village with no grand plan it has endearing informality and feels little changed.

James Stirling, a renowned mathematician, was a popular and forward thinking mine manager. He improved the efficiency of the mines through radical improvements to living and working conditions of the miners including limiting the working week to 40 hours over 6 days and allowing the building of houses and the cultivation of gardens.

Stirling, with the help of Allan Ramsay, the Pentland poet and native of Leadhills, formed Scotland's oldest subscription library in 1741. The library is on Main Street and is still in use as a reference library.

The improvement in living conditions may account for how one local resident, John Taylor, managed to live for 137 years – according to his gravestone anyway.

Another local lad made good was William Symington, an engineer, who designed and built the first steam engine propelled boat. He was unfortunately ahead of his time and died penniless – an obelisk to his memory overlooks the village.

At the centre of the village hanging from pyramidal supports is the curfew bell – dated 1770. The bell would peel the change of shifts and emergencies in the mines. Nowadays it is rung to bring in New Year and raise the alarm when a walker goes missing in the hills.

Hopetoun Arm hotel   37 Main Street   01659 74234

THIEF SLACK HASS (big loop)
It was through this pass that the Caledonian railway chose to build the highest railway line in the UK in 1900. The transportation of lead continued until 1930 and passengers were carried until 1939 when the line was closed. The summit of the pass at 404 metres is just out of Leadhills and is followed by a long steady descent to Elvanfoot.

Rail enthusiasts have re-opened the line between Leadhills and Wanlockhead and offer trips throughout the summer months – www.leadhillsrailway.co.uk

DALVEEN PASS (big loop)
This is not the highest of the passes but it is certainly the deepest and perhaps the most dramatic. There is little height to be gained from Elvanfoot but over 100 metres is lost in a thrilling descent.

As you approach the pass the wide open moor rises into hills and crowd up around the road. Ahead the steep green slopes of Steygail appear to block the way.

Turning into the pass small rocks spill off the very steep hillside to your left and on the right is a deep ravine – a particularly sunless spot occupied by the solitary Dalveen cottage.

Also on the left deep clefts, known as cleuchs, funnel energetic stream and destabilising gusts towards the road. In short the Dalveen pass is as spectacular as any Highland glen.

DRUMLANRIG CASTLE (big loop)

Built of red sandstone Drumlanrig Castle is a very grand and striking building – its nickname locally is the Pink Palace. Completed in the 1680s for the duke of Queensberry it remains the seat of the current duke of Buccleuch and Queensberry.

The castle is home to a renowned art collection and a notable cycle museum. There is also an extensive garden and woodland walks to explore.

A tearoom and snack bar sell locally produced food. More information at www.drumlanrig.com or contact on 01848 600 283.

SANQUHAR (both loops)

Stretched out along the A76 Sanquhar is a town with a history stretching back to 8th century. There is a ruined castle on its western edge and the town's museum is housed in a 17th century William Adam designed tollbooth.

Hardline Covenanters Richard Cameron, James Renwick and Donald Cargill attached their defiant declaration of Sanquhar to the tollbooth in 1680. The declaration denounced their allegiance to King Charles II. One month later Cameron was killed at the battle of Airds Moss. Both Cargill and Renwick were hunted down and executed at the gallows in Edinburgh for their continued defiance.

Sanquhar's post office is the oldest in the world and from where Robert Burns posted "Ae fond kiss" to his lover Clarinda.

Burnside Tea Room	Glasgow Road	016592 50328
Harvey's	3-4 Harvey's Wynd	016592 50955

CRAWICK PASS (both loops)

The Crawick pass is the most gentle and often the loneliest of the hill passes. The 100 metres of ascent between Sanquhar and Crawfordjohn is drawn out over 13 miles and is for the most part imperceptible.

As you cycle north encountering no more than isolated farms it is easy to understand what Dorothy Wordsworth meant when she wrote, "So many inhabited solitudes" in her journal of the tour of Scotland she undertook with her brother William, and poet Samuel Coleridge.

WANLOCKHEAD (wee loop)

Wanlockhead is Scotland's highest village. It sits in a hollow formed by the highest of the Lowther hills. The houses rise up the sides but don't quite mange to spill out. On sunny days the village is a very appealing place, however in winter the cold air sinks into the hollow and snow is common as early as October.

Wanlockhead is also a former mining village. There is a museum of lead mining, which includes an opportunity to go down the Loch Nell mine, pan for gold, browse the miners' library and experience a typical miner's cottage.

It is, however, enough to wander the old track beds and to view the old beam engine that pumped water from the mines.

| Wanlockhead Inn | Garden Dyke | 01659 74535 |
| Museum of Lead Mining | Goldscaur Row | 01659 74387 |

MENNOCK PASS (wee loop)
Early travellers in the Lowthers reported a feeling of claustrophobia when passing through and nowhere is this more apparent than in the Mennock pass.

This is also the most atmospheric of the passes and the steepness and proximity of the hills gives it enough grandeur to compete with any Highland glen.

The descent from Wanlockhead is very fast and thrilling. There are many twists and turns in the road and if you are too fast it can be difficult to maintain a safe line of descent without crossing to the wrong side of the road.

THE BIG LOOP ROUTE

	Grid ref.	Miles
1.	881 239	0

Start: village hall, Crawfordjohn.
Leave car park and go to the left through village. At 4 way junction turn downhill to the left and leave Crawfordjohn. Climb over the Apache pass and descend to junction with B797.

| 2. | 892 153 | 3 |

Turn right and follow B797 uphill into Leadhills

| 3. | 886 153 | 6 |

Take first left in Leadhills, signed B7040; Elvanfoot 5 miles. Follow B7040 to junction with A702.

| 4. | 951 174 | 11 |

Turn right onto the A702 at Elvanfoot. Once through the Dalveen pass continue to third right after Durisdeermill

| 5. | 874 000 | 25 |

Turn right, signed – Drumlanrig Castle 2. Follow to crossroads with A76. Cross A76 and follow road downhill, signed Drumlanrig Castle 1. Cross bridge over Nith and turn right, and follow curving road uphill.

6.   864 001   27

To visit Drumlanrig Castle continue along tree-lined drive for 150 yards. To continue with route turn right uphill, signed for the Estates Work Dept. The road climbs steeply onto a high ridge of land. Descent to Nith is thrilling but beware of T-junction beyond cottage – continue downhill. Follow the Nith upstream.

7.   804 082   37

When presented with a second opportunity to cross Nith at Mennock turn left and follow road to T-junction.

8.   774 096   40

Turn right and go towards Sanquhar parish church through industrial estate.

9.   773 108   40 1/2

Turn left at the Burnside Tearoom and follow A76 for a short distance out of Sanquhar over narrow bridge (traffic lights).

10.   774 107   41

Once over bridge turn right, signed B740, Crawfordjohn 13. At Crawfordjohn turn right into village to return to start.

11.   881 239   54

End: village hall, Crawfordjohn (see map page 14)

THE WEE LOOP ROUTE AND THE MENNOCK PASS.

The small loop continues through Leadhills at point 3 and continues to follow the B797 through Wanlockhead and into the Mennock Pass. At the junction with A76 turn right and then after 1/2 mile turn left over the Nith to take up big loop route at point 7.

The Dalveen Pass

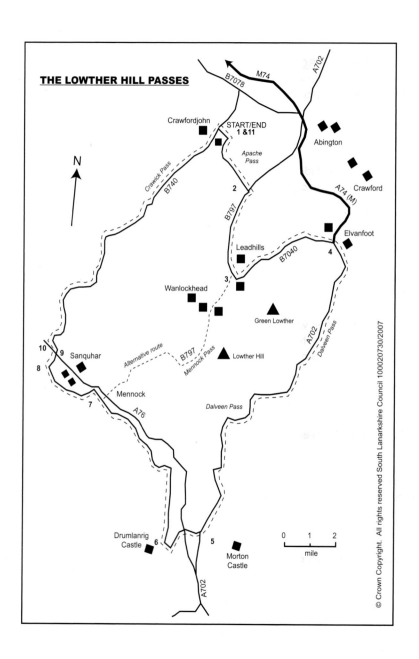

THE LOWTHER HILL PASSES

B7078
M74
A702

Crawfordjohn

START/END
1 &11

Apache
Pass

Abington

Crawick Pass
B740

Crawford

A74 (M)

2

B797

Elvanfoot

Leadhills

B7040

4

3

Wanlockhead

Green Lower

A702

Dalveen Pass

10
9 Sanquhar

Alternative route
B797
Mennock Pass

Lowther Hill

8

7

Mennock

A76

Dalveen Pass

Drumlanrig
Castle
6

5

Morton
Castle

0   1   2
mile

A702

THE LOWTHER OFF-ROAD ODYSSEY – 55 MILES

This extensive route links ancient rights-of-way, forestry roads and an abandoned railway line to form a 55-mile circular route that starts and finishes in Douglas.

It is possible to complete the route in a single day however a more relaxed trip over two days with an overnight in Leadhills or Wanlockhead is a better bet.

It was impractical to include maps of this route however you can download a digital version of the route at www.outdoor-clydesdale.com

DOUGLAS TO SANQUHAR

Distance: 17 miles
Grade: hard
Terrain: initially this route follows tarmac roads. It also climbs through over 300 feet in the first five miles. At Auchendaff, with most of the height gained, the route then follows fairly level grassy tracks. Three fords, which can be deep at times, need to be negotiated.

After a short soft section with no obvious path the route joins good forestry roads. There follows two thrilling downhill sections with a climb to over 1500 feet in between. The final downhill into Sanquhar is on a little used tarmac road.

There are off-road alternatives to following the A70 out of Douglas that are obvious from the map. However these options require patience and persistence.

Map: OS Landranger sheet 71

By the way

Despite the occasional signs of life and the signs that point the way this is a very lonely route over the high moors between the Clyde and the Nith. A route like this developed because ancient travellers would rather brave the exposure and the elements on the moor than run the risk of ambush in the Clyde valley.

For more information on DOUGLAS – see page 67 and for Sanquhar – see page 11

THE ROUTE

	Grid ref.	Miles
1.	835 308	0

Start: Main Street, Douglas.

From Main Street turn right onto Ayr Road. Follow Ayr Road west out of Douglas.

| 2. | 821 287 | 2 |

Two miles out of Douglas turn left. Follow red road for a mile or so to a T-junction.

| 3. | 816 271 | 3 |

At T-junction turn to left. After crossing over conveyor belt turn right, signed Glentaggart 1 1/2 . Follow red road ever more up hill onto open moor.

| 4. | 794 235 | 6 |

At end of surfaced road continue straight-on towards Auchendaff farm.

| 5. | 785 236 | 6 1/2 |

Sign indicates Sanquhar 12 miles to left. Take up grassy track that runs back the way past rusty shed and around sheep pens and then continues towards small conifer plantation.

| 6. | 765 227 | 7 1/2 |

Three fords have to be negotiated. Beyond third ford climb over gate follow track over soft marshy ground along edge of forest. After 200 yards the surface improves; continue straight on with forest on your left and open valley to your right and follow to T-junction.

| 7. | 755 223 | 8 1/2 |

Turn left at T-junction and follow good forestry road south west.

| 8. | 738 203 | 10 |

Signpost indicates Sanquhar 6, Wanlockhead 12 1/2 to the left; and Muirkirk 6 – to the right. Go left for Sanquhar. Follow good forestry road out of trees and downhill to Fingland.

| 9. | 754 176 | 12 |

At Fingland go to the right, signed Kirkconnel 5, Sanquhar 6. Join the road to Sanquhar and undertake long uphill to over 1500 feet followed by long and thrilling downhill into Sanquhar.

| 10. | 775 112 | 17 |

At junction with B740 go straight over and cross iron bridge. Turn right for Sanquhar. Turn left to continue with route – see below for Sanquhar to Wanlockhead section.

SANQUHAR TO WANLOCKHEAD/LEADHILLS

Distance: 15 miles

Grade: hard

Terrain: the climb starts immediately and is very steep in places. The first few miles are on tarmac.

Off-road the trend is uphill with many steep sections. There are short downhills and a couple of reasonably long level sections on which to recover. The off-road surface is a little loose to begin with but in the main the route follows good forest roads – although these can be greasy at times.

Map: OS Landranger sheet 71

By the way

A straightforward if rather circuitous route that offers good views from the first high point high above the Crawick pass before turning east into tree filled glens.

Wanlockhead at 1531 feet and Leadhills at 1295 feet are Scotland's highest villages. Both communities are very redolent of their lead mining past and offer an authentic insight into the lives of miners and their families. For more information on Wanlockhead see page 11 and for Leadhills see page 9.

THE ROUTE

	Grid ref.	Miles
11.	776 109	17

Once over iron bridge turn left past row of cottages and continue under viaduct. Follow steep road uphill to T-junction and turn left. Continue with moderate climb.

12.	800 115	19

Follow road to left past tumbledown cottage for Clenries. Continue to climb. At Clenries farm continue straight on, signed Cogshead 9 km. Join rough road. Track levels out. Good view to north up Crawick valley. Continue past telecom building.

13.	806 147	21

Signpost indicates Cogheads 5 km to the right. Follow to the right and then follow forestry road through gate and uphill into trees. Continue straight on at ruined cottage at Cogshead ignoring signs for Southern Upland Way. Follow forestry road to T-junction.

14.	832 157	26

At T-junction turn right indicated by yellow SUW arrow. Forestry road eventually leaves trees and sweeps downhill past Duntercleuch and then levels out by Wanlock Water. Track eventually joins surfaced road. Follow surfaced road into Wanlockhead.

15.	879 132	32

Climb through Wanlockhead, taking left fork past Wanlockhead Inn and hostel to junction with B797. Turn right onto B797 and climb for a short distance before descending into Leadhills.

WANLOCKHEAD/LEADHILLS TO CRAWFORDJOHN AND DOUGLAS

Distance: 23 miles

Grade: hard

Terrain: the track bed of the old Caledonian railway offers a gradual descent from Leadhills except for a deep dip once bridged by the now demolished Rispingcluech viaduct. The surface is in the main very good.

The second off-road section can be soft and the route is obscure in sections on the uphill. On the downhill the surface is grassy or of hard standing. There are three fords to negotiate – one of which can be deep. The final section is either on road or a tarmac cycle-path with a short section of good tracks through the Douglas castle policies.

Map: OS Landranger sheets 71 and 78

By the way

A short distance out of Leadhills the route follows the track bed of the old Caledonian railway, which linked Leadhills and Wanlockhead to the west coast main line at Elvanfoot. The line was opened in 1900 to carry lead and passengers but was closed in 1938 when commercial lead mining more or less came to an end.

The route home passes through the ancient village of Crawfordjohn (see page 25) and the Douglas castle policies. Douglas castle – only a ruined tower remains – is often referred to as Castle Dangerous because it and the ruthless actions of the 'Good' Sir James Douglas who surprised the English garrison while they were at church on Palm Sunday 1304 inspired Sir Walter Scott's book Castle Dangerous.

THE ROUTE

	Grid ref.	Miles
16.	887 153	33

In Leadhills turn right, signed – B7040, Elvanfoot 5.

17.	896 150	33 1/2

After short climb join rough track off to the left close to top of the pass. This is the track bed of the old Caledonian railway. Follow track bed gently downhill except for dip where viaduct has been removed.

18.	934 176	37

After 3 miles it is necessary to rejoin the road. Follow road to T-junction.

19.	951 174	38

Turn left at T-junction. After 500 yards just beyond Elvanfoot farm leave road and join obvious track. Don't go to right but continue uphill past mobile phone transmitter. Track is soft but good until it encounters the Collins burn. From here the grass is long and the track is difficult to detect. Cross burn and take up faint track on far side. Maybe easier to push to gate at top of shallow pass.

20.	942 194	39 1/2

Better track sweeps downhill toward M74 below. Track then goes round to left away from motorway and follows pylons into next glen. Track descends to cross Glencaple burn. Climb away from burn to fork in tracks.

21.	923 210	41

Take high track off to the left and follow round hillside to avoid Glencaple farm. Follow track downhill through two fords. Track levels out. Continue to ford at Lettershaws caravan site.

22.	903 206	42 1/2

Negotiate ford, which can be deep – bridge available 50 yards downstream – avoid caravan site. On far side of burn follow track to B797.

23.	902 207	

Turn left onto B797. Follow B797 for about one mile.

24.   **895 194**   **43 1/2**

Turn right uphill to follow road uphill over Apache pass. Follow road to Crawfordjohn.

25.   **879 238**   **46 1/2**

At junction in Crawfordjohn join B740 and follow to the right to junction with cycle-path and B7078.

26.   **891 260**   **48**

Turn left onto cycle-path and follow north to junction with A70.

27.   **856 326**   **53**

At junction with A70 cross to far side and follow track downhill to locked gate. Cross gate and follow good track through mature parkland. Take second right downhill and follow track by small loch west into Douglas.

28.   **835 308**   **55**

End: Main Street, Douglas.

One of the many fords on the first leg of the odyssey.

ABINGTON, CRAWFORD AND THE CAMPS RESERVOIR

This is a relaxing route that is ideal for a family cycle trip. From Abington it follows a minor road now closed to through traffic. The road to, and the rough road around the Camps reservoir takes you deep into the Lowther hills where you will encounter few cars. For variety you can opt to return via the cycle lane by the A702. However retracing your outward route is the more pleasant option.

Distance: up to 17 miles
Grade: easy
Terrain: there is a short climb out of Abington, another to reach the level of the reservoir and there is a small hump to be overcome on the way round the reservoir. The road from Abington can be a bit rough in places but the road surface out to the reservoir is excellent. The road around the reservoir is unsurfaced however it is generally level and in very good condition.
Map: OS Landranger sheet 72.

By the way

ABINGTON

Abington is a pleasant village and seems to suffer few ill effects from being sandwiched between the west coast main line and the M74. Established in the 19th century by the politically influential Colebrook family the overall impression is one of uniformity.

Abington Hotel, Carlisle Road – 01864 502 467; Welcome Break, Junction 13, M74; Abington general store and tearoom, 85-87 Carlisle Road – 01864 502 374.

CASTLE CRAWFORD

Castle Crawford or the Lindsay tower, as it is sometimes known, was built in the 16th century on the site of an earlier motte. Set among tall trees it is in a ruinous and dangerous state.

The castle was at one time a royal castle and in 1537 it was the venue for a dinner in honour of the French ambassador given by King James V. The ambassador was in Scotland because James V was about to marry his first wife Magdalene of France. At the meal the guests were presented with cups full of gold bonnet pieces; the gold having been mined from the nearby Crawford moor.

THE CAMPS RESERVOIR

The reservoir road takes you away from the biz of the Clyde valley and by the time you reach the reservoir you are completely enveloped by hills.

The dam holding back the reservoir blends in well with its surroundings. Early work on the dam was carried out by German prisoners of war captured road during the First

World War. The Geneva Convention eventually banned such exploitation of captive soldiers. Running alongside the road out to the reservoir the bed of railway track that carried construction materials out to the dam can still be detected.

Archaeologists have unearthed evidence of Bronze Age cemeteries and cremation sites and signs of settlement on the hillsides all round the reservoir.

The Midlock valley, the left fork just beyond Midlock farm, provides an entertaining alternative to the trip around the reservoir. The road is rough in places but it offers more variety as it twists and turns while hugging the sides of this narrow valley. The view to the head of the valley is terrific and nearly always visible.

CRAWFORD

Crawford is an ancient settlement: the Roman's built a large fort nearby and Robert II elevated it to a burgh of Barony in 1370 giving it the right to hold markets.

Strung out along what used to be the main road north to south Crawford has always been a well-used staging post. The Crawford Inn had many famous patrons including Sir Robert Peel, Henry, duke of Bordeaux (rightful heir to the French crown) and Prince Louis Napoleon Bonaparte.

With the arrival of the railway the village became a popular tourist destination despite its position at over 900 feet above sea level and being known for being a very cold spot. Easily reached from both Glasgow and Edinburgh it was a popular day trip for anglers and those wishing to picnic by the Clyde.

Barry's Corner Shop (snacks)   83 Carlisle Road, Crawford   01864 502595

THE ROUTE

	Grid ref.	Miles
1.	932 233	0

Start: car park to the rear of the Royal Bank of Scotland, Abington.
Leave car park as directed and turn left downhill. Cross bridge over Clyde and the climb up and over railway line.

2.	937 232	1/4

Turn right at T-junction and follow quiet lane that runs alongside the railway line. Follow to T-junction.

3.	953 214	3 3/4

Turn left at T-junction and follow road past Castle Crawford to fork in road just beyond Midlock farm.

4.	951 215	4 1/2

Take left fork for Camps reservoir (right fork for Midlock valley and Welphill).
Follow level road but stop before descending into small settlement at foot of dam. Maintain your height by continuing onto rough road behind houses. Go through gate and follow rough road to rejoin road climbing to reservoir.

5.   **001 224**   **7 1/2**

Follow road around reservoir in either direction (4 miles). Anti-clockwise leaves the short climb to the end. Retrace outward route but continue into Crawford to T-junction.

6.   **953 211**   **14**

Turn right at T-junction and continue to roundabout.

7.   **946 205**   **14 1/2**

Join cycle lane that circumnavigates the roundabout and take exit, signed Abington A702. Follow cycle lane into Abington.

8.   **932 233**   **17**

End: Royal Bank of Scotland, Abington. (see map page 24)

A good picnic spot overlooking Crawford.

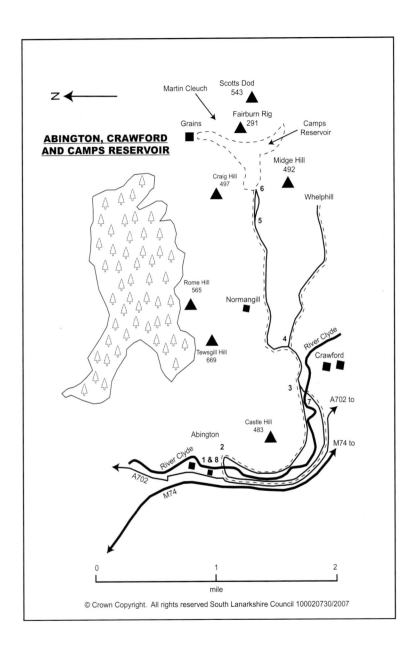

ABINGTON, CRAWFORD
AND CAMPS RESERVOIR

N

Martin Cleuch

Scotts Dod
543 ▲

Fairburn Rig
291 ▲

Grains
■

Camps
Reservoir

Midge Hill
492 ▲

Craig Hill
497 ▲

6

Whelphill

5

Rome Hill
565 ▲

Normangill
■

Tewsgill Hill
669 ▲

4

River Clyde

Crawford
■ ■

3

7

A702 to

Castle Hill
483 ▲

M74 to

Abington

2

River Clyde

1 & 8
■

A702

M74

0   1   2

mile

THE DUNEATON VALLEY AND CRAWFORDJOHN

This circular excursion to the north of Abington follows the national cycle route for a short distance before heading into the very peaceful Duneaton valley to the medieval settlement of Crawfordjohn.

Distance: 10 miles
Grade: moderate
Terrain: it is a gradual climb from Abington to Crawfordjohn and it pauses frequently. The return route between Crawfordjohn and the cycle path involves a moderate climb.
Map: OS Landranger sheet 72

By the way
CRAWFORDJOHN

Crawfordjohn occupies the only truly habitable spot between a wide expanse of moorland that stretches away to the north and the Lowther hills to the south.
An ecclesiastical site since medieval times and a barony since 1688, it was the preferred base of the Cameronians, the Covenanter regiment, after the settlement of 1690.

Colebrooke Arms 7 Main Street 01864 504239

THE ROUTE

	Grid ref.	Miles
1.	**932 233**	**0**

Start: car park to the rear if the Royal Bank of Scotland.
Leave car park as directed and turn right, then right again and follow the main thoroughfare out of the village to the roundabout.

2. **931 247** **3/4**
At rounabout join the cycle lane and follow signs for Douglas B7078 uphill over the M74.

3. **928 246** **1**
At second roundabout follow the cycle lane and then cross the B7078 to join the traffic free cycle path. Cycle path rises and then descends gently to left turn – signed Crawfordjohn 3 3/4.

4. **918 249** **1 3/4**
Take left for Crawfordjohn. Follow undulating road running parallel to the Duneaton Water.

5. **897 240** **4 1/4**
Once over bridge turn left onto Manse Road and follow uphill into Crawfordjohn.

6. **879 238** **5 1/4**
At 4 way junction on far side of Crawfordjohn turn right, signed – B740, Abington 5. Follow road to B7078.

7.   891 259   7

Turn right and rejoin cycle-path and follow south to roundabout. Take up cycle lane and cross B7078 – follow to conclusion at second roundabout and return to Abington.

8.   932 233   10

End: Royal Bank of Scotland, Abington.

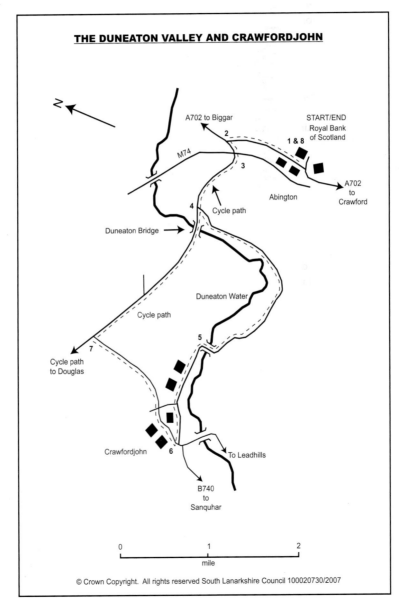

THE DUNEATON VALLEY AND CRAWFORDJOHN

A702 to Biggar

2

START/END
Royal Bank
of Scotland

1 & 8

M74

3

A702
to
Crawford

Abington

4

Cycle path

Duneaton Bridge

Duneaton Water

Cycle path

5

Cycle path
to Douglas

7

Crawfordjohn

6

To Leadhills

B740
to
Sanquhar

0   1   2
mile

Bike Lanarkshire

THE DAER RESERVOIR

Distance: A702 to foot of dam – 3 miles; A702 to Kirkhope farm - 6 miles
Grade: easy/moderate
Terrain: the only significant hill is between the bottom and the top of the dam.
Getting there: leave the M74 at junction 14 and follow A702 south, signed – Thornhill and Drumlanrig Castle. Follow A702 for three miles beyond Elvanfoot. Road to Daer reservoir is on the right _ mile beyond car park for Glenochar heritage trail.

By the way

This is a ride of two halves. The first is an undemanding cycle to the foot of the dam where there are good spots to picnic. Beyond the steep pull to the top of the dam the countryside is remote and empty.

The road ends at Kirkhope farm at a seemingly unsustainably remote location. Queensbury Hill the highest point on the horizon beyond the farm is now regarded as the source of the Clyde.

THE ROUTE

	Grid ref.	Miles
1.	951 133	0

Start: junction of A702 and the road to the reservoir, signed – Daer waterworks.

2.	972 097	3

At junction turn right and descend to bridge. Road climbs to top of dam – steeply at times. Road is more or less level to Kirkhope farm.

3.	963 054	6

Road end, Kirkhope farm. (see map page 28)

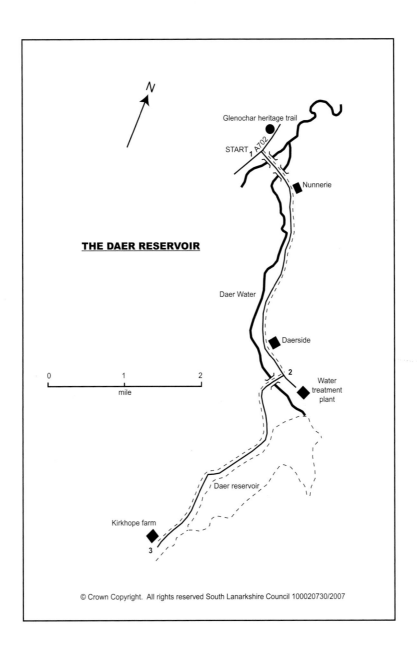

THE DAER RESERVOIR

Glenochar heritage trail

START A702

Nunnerie

Daer Water

Daerside

2

Water treatment plant

0   1   2

mile

Daer reservoir

Kirkhope farm

3

THE BIGGAR ROUTES

BIGGAR

Biggar is an open and inviting town that nestles on a high plain between the rivers Clyde and Tweed. Its wide medieval High Street bristles with activity. For a town made a burgh of barony in 1451 it seems peculiarly vulnerable to attack but perhaps congeniality was its defence. Several Scottish sovereigns are known to have enjoyed hunting in the area while staying at Boghall castle.

The feudal lords of Biggar were the Flemings. The Flemings occupied Boghall castle and were responsible for the building of the town's St Mary's Church in 1545 – the last collegiate church to be built in Scotland.

A Fleming daughter, Mary, was chosen to accompany the young Mary Queen of Scots to France in 1548. At the annual Biggar gala day a local girl is crowned the Fleming Queen a tradition inspired by the association with Mary Queen of Scots.

Biggar is a town that takes its heritage seriously. Five museums are to be found in the town and all but one are maintained and run by the voluntary Bigagar Museum Trust. The trust is also responsible for Brownsbank cottage, the last home of poet Hugh MacDairmaid at nearby Candy Mill and the John Buchan centre in Broughton.

BIGGAR MUSEUMS

Moat Park heritage centre: a display of models that illustrate Clydesdale's geological formation and in particular the area's Roman and Iron Age history. Housed in a former church it also contains the impressive Moffat Menzies tapestry.

Gladstone Court: a hands on museum that recreates the 19th century. A Victorian street with typical shops and a Victorian schoolroom are also part of the experience.

The Albion museum and archive: the Albion motor company was started with a bond on a local farm. The museum exploits the link and has a few vintage Albion vehicles on display. It also houses the Albion archive – that is the complete records of the Albion Motor company.

Greenhill Covenanters' House: this 17th century house was built in its original location near Wiston on the south side of Tinto during the Killing Times – a bloody period when people who supported the National Covenant and its aim of defending the Presbyterian form of worship were hunted down by government troops and often summarily executed. The museum tries to shed some light on this period and has a copy of the National Covenant signed in 1638.

Gasworks Museum (National Museum of Scotland): built in 1839 the Biggar gasworks are the only preserved gasworks in Scotland.

GETTING THERE

From Edinburgh follow the A702 from the centre of Edinburgh for 29 miles. From Glasgow leave the M74 at junction 7, Larkhall and follow the A72 Clyde valley tourist route to Lanark. From Lanark follow the A73 over the Hyndford bridge, then take the left to rejoin the A72 after about four miles for Symington and Biggar. Follow all the way to the A702 and then turn left for Biggar.

From the south leave the M74 at junction 13, Abington and follow the A702(T) north for 12 miles to Biggar via Lamington and Coulter.

EATING AND DRINKING

Biggar (01899 -)

55	55 High Street	221555
The Golden Fry chip shop	110 High Street	220133
Taj Mahal	101 High Street	220801
The Oriental	3 Park Place	221894
The Crown	109 High Street	220116
Cross Keys	1 High Street	220176
Townhead Cafe	187 High Street	221001
The Coffee Spot	152 High Street	221092
The Gillespie Centre	75 High Street	220994

EATING, DRINKING AND STAYING

Biggar (01899 -)

Elphinstone Hotel	145 High Street	220044
Shieldhill Castle Hotel	Shieldhill Road, Quothquan	220035
Cornhill House	Coulter	220001
Clydesdale Hotel	76 High Street	221100
Skirling House	Skirling by Biggar	860274

STAYING

Biggar (01899 -)

Daleside B&B	165 High Street	220097
Hartree House	Station Road	229108
Cormiston Farm Cottage	Cormiston Road	220200
Glen Avon B&B	2A Boghall Avenue	220954
Larchfield	Hartree Road	220726

OUWITH BIGGAR (01899 -)

Dunsyre Mains Farm	810251
Walston House	308697
Walston Mansion Farmhouse	810334

BIGGAR, DUNSYRE AND NEWBIGGING

This route climbs out of Biggar into the Pentland Hills and to the head of the Medwin valley to the hamlet of Dunsyre. Very few people visit this corner of the otherwise very popular Pentlands. The roads are consequently delightfully peaceful.

Distance: 23 miles
Grade: moderate/hard
Terrain: the route starts with a long gradual climb. The road in the Pentlands is, in the main, gently undulating. The trend toward Dunsyre is downhill and towards Newbigging the trend is uphill.
Map: OS Landranger sheet 72

BY THE WAY

WALSTON
The hamlet of Walston sits at the foot of the Black Mount. The church dates from the 17th century and there are some good examples of portrait headstones from the early 18th century.

NEWHOLM
This private house near Dunsyre was the home of General Learmouth – the commander of the Covenanter horsemen at the battle of Rullion Green in 1666. The Covenanters were roundly beaten and Learmouth was forced into hiding. He would evade his pursuers by the way of a secret passage that led away from the house to the banks of the Medwin.

DUNSYRE
A pretty hamlet with an ancient churchyard. William Somervil, a former minister at Dunsyre and signatory of National Covenant in 1638 is buried there.

The present church dates from the 19th century but a set of jougs have been preserved and set into the wall. To be placed in the jougs, the equivalent of the stocks, was a humiliating and uncomfortable punishment for behaviour deemed unacceptable to the church.

The jougs were placed around the offenders neck and are set in the wall at such a height that it was neither comfortable to sit or stand.

LITTLE SPARTA
One mile beyond Dunsyre is Little Sparta, the home of the late poet Dr Ian Hamilton Findlay. In his remarkable garden Findlay expressed his poetry in a concrete form. Works include Nuclear Sail and Air Craft Carrier bird table (check sign for opening times).

NEWBIGGING

Look out for the distinctly pagan mercat cross which dates from 1693.

Nestlers Inn   01555 840860

QUOTHQUAN

The Shieldhill Hotel was once the home of the Chancellor family. However the family had to live in the old tower from 1528 when their mansion house was burned down for supporting Mary Queen of Scots at the battle of Langside. The replacement was built in the 18th century and is now the hotel.

At the far end of Quothquan, just beyond the fork in the road, is the ruin of the old kirk. The Chancellors are buried in the aisle.

Shieldhill Castle Hotel   01899 220035

CULTER MOTTE HILL

An early defensive site probably constructed by early Norman settlers in the 11th and 12th centuries. At first it seems an unlikely place for a defensive installation but once on top you can appreciate the uninterrupted view up and down the Clyde and through to the Tweed.

THE ROUTE

	Grid ref.	Miles
1.	043 379	0

Start: Biggar Corn Exchange
Turn left onto High street and after 100 yards turn right, signed Carnwath B7016. Climb past the Moat Park heritage centre and continue out of Biggar.

| 2. | 041 390 | 1 |

Road forks ahead. Take the right hand fork, signed Elsrickle 3. Follow undulating road to crossroads with A721.

| 3. | 055 430 | 4 |

Cross A721. Continue past school at Walston and follow road round to the right at next junction. Continue through Walston on gentle downhill.

| 4. | 083 472 | 8 |

At next junction turn left, signed - Dunsyre 1. Follow road through trees at Newholm, over small footbridge and through Dunsyre. Follow road all the way to Newbigging.

| 5. | 014 458 | 13 1/2 |

At T-junction with A721 in Newbigging turn left. Follow A721 downhill for about 1 mile.

6.   023 446   14 1/2

When the road bends and conifers line both sides of the road turn right, signed Biggar 4. Long uphill takes you over 1000 feet. Fast descent brings you to T-junction with B7016.

7.   028 410   16 1/2

Turn left on B7016 and follow for 100 yards. Turn right onto Shieldhill Road, signed – Thankerton 5, Quothquan 3. Follow level and tree-lined road past the Shieldhill Hotel to Quothquan.

8.   995 395   18 1/2

Road forks at far end of the hamlet of Quothquan by the red telephone box. Take left fork. Follow more or less level road to junction.

9.   003 396   20

Turn left at junction and continue through Cormiston. From Cormiston the road descends steeply.

10.   018 366   21

As road levels out turn left, signed – cycleway, (continuing straight on for 200 yards for Culter Motte Hill). Follow straight and level road into Biggar. At T-junction with High Street turn left to return to Corn Exchange.

11.   043 379   23

End: Corn Exchange.

TOUR OF BIGGAR COMMON.

A shorter circular tour of Biggar common (10 miles) can be undertaken by following the route as outlined below as far as point 2. However continue along the B7016 for a further mile and then take up route from point 8.

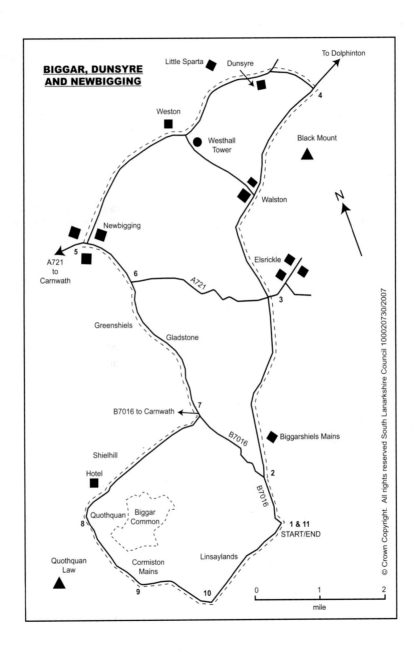

BIGGAR, DUNSYRE
AND NEWBIGGING

Little Sparta

Dunsyre

To Dolphinton

4

Weston

Westhall
Tower

Black Mount

Walston

N

Newbigging

A721
to
Carnwath

5

6

Elsrickle

3

A721

Greenshiels

Gladstone

B7016 to Carnwath

7

B7016

Biggarshiels Mains

Shielhill

Hotel

2

B7016

Quothquan

Biggar
Common

1 & 11
START/END

Quothquan
Law

Cormiston
Mains

Linsaylands

8

9

10

0   1   2

mile

BIGGAR, BROUGHTON, KILBUCHO AND COULTER

From Biggar to Broughton the countryside takes on a new quality. Throughout both legs of the route you are surrounded by graceful Border Hills.

Distance: 13 miles
Grade: moderate
Terrain: for much of this route the road is level or gently undulating. There is one short steepish climb on the way to Broughton. On the return both options involve a climb. The Kilbucho and Coulter route involves a sustained climb to over 1000 feet. The alternative involves a short but steep climb towards the end.
Map: OS Landranger sheet 72

BY THE WAY

BROUGHTON

A short detour along the road to the left as you enter Broughton leads to the churchyard. A plaque at the entrance explains that St Llolan or perhaps St Maurice, may have established a church here as early as the 7th century.

A vaulted chamber attached to the ruined church has been rather optimistically declared as St Llolan's cell. The key can be obtained from the village shop.

John Buchan author of the 39-steps holidayed with his family in Broughton and all around is the kind of scenery that may have inspired him to write his tales of adventure and pursuit. The John Buchan centre at the southern end of the village is devoted to the author and statesman's life. When Buchan became a life peer he chose the title baron Tweedsmuir.

Broughton also claims an association with King Arthur and Merlin. Close inspection of the OS map will reveal names such as Merlindale – the reputed final resting place of the poet/magician. Altarstone by the minor road over to Dreva is where St Kentigern is supposed to have baptised Merlin.

Laurel Bank Tearoom	Main Street	01899 830462
Broughton Store (snacks)	Main Street	01899 830465

THE ROUTE

	Grid ref.	Miles
1.	043 379	0

Start: Corn Exchange.

Turn right along High Street and after 300 yards turn right, signed – Broughton B7016. Follow this road all the way to T-junction with Main St, Broughton.

2.	113 367	5

Turn right, signed – Moffat A701. Proceed along Main Street.

3.	113 359	5 1/2

Just beyond the Greenmantle brewery take the next right, signed – Coulter 6, Hartree 5, Tweed cycleway. Follow road to fork at Kilbucho Place.

4.	096 353	6 1/2

Take left fork, signed - Coulter 5. Follow rising road to summit of pass at 1100 feet. Continue past right for Biggar and descend to next right. (For shorter and easier alternative take right fork just before you reach the top of the hill turn right, signed - Biggar 1 1/2; take up route from point 7 below).

5.	032 343	11

Take right (1/2 mile short of Coulter). Follow road to T-junction just beyond Thirpland Farm to T-junction.

6.	040 361	12

Turn left at T-junction and follow road to second T-junction.

7	042 362	13

Turn left and follow road into Biggar. Turn right at the end of Station Road to return to the Corn Exchange.

8.	043 379	13 1/4

End: Corn Exchange (see map page 38)

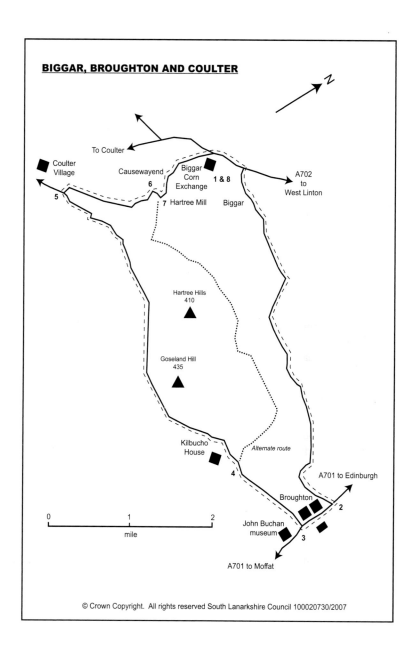

BIGGAR, BROUGHTON AND COULTER

N

To Coulter

Coulter
Village

Causewayend

Biggar
Corn
Exchange

1 & 8

A702
to
West Linton

6

5

7 Hartree Mill

Biggar

Hartree Hills
410

Goseland Hill
435

Kilbucho
House

Alternate route

4

A701 to Edinburgh

Broughton

2

0   1   2

mile

John Buchan
museum

3

A701 to Moffat

BIGGAR, SKIRLING, CANDY MILL AND ELSRICKLE

Distance: 14 miles
Grade: moderate
Terrain: There are several small climbs but nothing too sustained or difficult. The return from Elsrickle is delightful.
Map: OS Landranger sheet 72

This route follows undulating lanes where the cyclist can indulge in villages and countryside that reflects the popular perception of a rural idyll. There is a ford to tackle, leafy lanes to enjoy and fine views of Tinto on offer.

BY THE WAY
SKIRLING

With its village green Skirling has the definite feel of England rather than the Scottish Borders. Nevertheless the green is a very appealing innovation that should be replicated throughout Scotland.

The green is shaded by large broad-leaved trees and on three sides the green is lined by low cottages. On the fourth side is the main road and the village kirk. Contributing further to a country idyll is Skirling House built in 1908 for Lord Carmichael by an Arts and Crafts architect and is now an award winning B&B (see page 30).

It incorporates such features as brass lamps and a village pump.

Skirling was an important staging post for cattle drovers on their way to markets in Edinburgh and Lanark or maybe even one of Skirling's three annual fairs.

A short uphill takes you out of Skirling. On the following downhill control your speed if you want to avoid fording the river at its foot; there is a footbridge to the right of the ford.

CANDY MILL AND BROWNSBANK COTTAGE

Brownsbank cottage was the home of poet Hugh MacDairmaid (Christopher Grieve) from 1952 until his death in 1978. MacDairmaid's best known work is the poem, A drunk man looks at the thistle. The cottage is maintained by the Biggar Museum Trust and visits are by appointment only, contact the museum trust on, 01899 221050

Between Candy and Elsrickle is the ruined Edmonston High House. This may have been the home of the 4th earl of Morton, regent to the young King James IV.

Morton is said to have introduced the guillotine to Scotland and the first to test its function.

ELSRICKLE

An exposed village strung out along the A721. The silhouette of the church on the horizon is stark.

QUOTHQUAN

The Shieldhill Hotel was once the home of the Chancellor family. However the family had to live in the old tower from 1528 when their mansion house was burned down for supporting Mary Queen of Scots at the battle of Langside. The replacement was built in the 18th century and is now the hotel.

At the far end of Quothquan, just beyond the fork in the road, is the ruin of the old kirk. The Chancellors are buried in the aisle.

Shieldhill Castle Hotel   01899 220035

CULTER MOTTE HILL

An early defensive site probably constructed by early Norman settlers in the 11th and 12th centuries. At first it seems an unlikely place for a defensive installation but once on top you can appreciate the uninterrupted view up and down the Clyde and through to the Tweed.

Fording the burn at Candy Mill

THE ROUTE

	Grid ref.	Miles
1.	043 379	0

Start: Corn Exchange, Biggar.

Turn right along High Street. After 300 yards turn right, signed – Broughton. Follow this road uphill out of Biggar.

2.	068 378	1 1/2

About 1 mile out of Biggar take left at bottom of fast downhill, signed – Skirling _ mile. Follow narrow lane to T-junction with A72.

3.	074 388	2 1/4

Turn right onto A72 and cycle through village of Skirling to large war memorial on traffic island.

4.	076 393	2 1/2

Turn left at war memorial and climb away from Skirling. Road then turns steeply downhill to ford through Candy Burn. Approach ford slowly as road surface is cobbled. Footbridge alternative. Short climb to A702.

5.	065 033	3 1/2

Turn right onto A702 and follow for 1/2 mile. Leave A702 at next left, unsigned. Follow undulating road to junction with A721 at Elsrickle.

6.	059 432	5 1/2

Turn left onto A721. Follow for short distance and take next left. Fast descent follows – DO NOT CYCLE TO BOTTOM OF HILL. Take next right and follow level road to next T-junction.

7.	029 410	8

Turn left onto B7016. After 100 yards turn right onto Shieldhill Road, signed – Thankerton 5, Quothquan 3 . Follow level and tree-lined road past the Shieldhill Hotel to Quothquan.

8.	995 395	10

Road forks at far end of the hamlet of Quothquan by the red telephone box. Follow more or less level road to junction.

9.	003 396	11 1/2

Turn left at junction and continue through Cormiston. From Cormiston the road descends steeply.

10.	018 366	12 1/2

As road levels out turn left, signed – cycleway, (continue straight on for 200 yards for Culter Motte Hill). Follow straight and level road into Biggar. At T-junction with High Street turn left to return to Corn Exchange.

11.	043 370	14 1/2

End: Corn Exchange. (see map page 42)

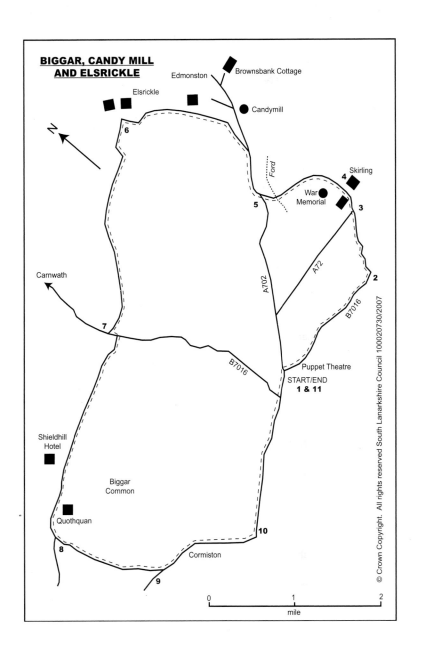

BIGGAR, CANDY MILL
AND ELSRICKLE

Edmonston

Brownsbank Cottage

Elsrickle

Candymill

N

6

Ford

Skirling

4

War
Memorial

5

3

Carnwath

A702

A72

2

B7016

7

© Crown Copyright. All rights reserved South Lanarkshire Council 1000207730/2007

B7016

Puppet Theatre

START/END
1 & 11

Shieldhill
Hotel

Biggar
Common

Quothquan

10

8

Cormiston

9

0   1   2

mile

THE COVENANTER'S GRAVE (off road)

This off-road and evocative route follows a Roman road that was still in use as the Biggar to Edinburgh turnpike until the 18th century. On the outward leg you are cycling in the footsteps of Covenanters on their way to the battle of Rullion Green. The return route follows their retreat into the Pentland Hills and visits the grave of one of Covenanters who did not make it home.

Distance: 12
Grade: moderate
Terrain: other than an initial climb the route between Dolphinton and the golf course is more or less level. There are two short steep sections on the return where the bike can be pushed if necessary. The grave lies to the north of the track on open hillside near the summit of Black Law and will require some expertise in off-road cycling to reach it. It is however an easy walk.

Map: OS Explorer sheets 336 & 344

BY THE WAY

In November 1666 a growing army of Covenanters marched along the old road between Biggar and Edinburgh. Ill-equipped and with no apparent support in Edinburgh the 1000 strong force attempted to retreat into the south-west of Scotland.

The retreating Covenanters were however intercepted by General Tam Dalyell and 3000 well-trained government troops at Rullion Green near Penicuik. A rout ensued and the surviving Covenanters fled across the Pentland hills.

One badly injured Covenanter reached shepherd Adam Sanderson's cottage at Blackhill. It is not clear whether he sought help and refused it or if he was urged to move by Sanderson in fear of reprisals. The low remaining walls of the cottage can be seen from the track when it dips to cross the Medwin Water.

Sanderson was aware that the dying Covenanter was desperate to reach a point from where he could glimpse the Ayrshire hills of home just one last time.

The next day Sanderson found him dead. At great personal risk he transported his body high onto the moors a little way short of the summit of Black Law and from here you can indeed see the Ayshire hills.

Archaeologists excavated the grave and found the Covenanters well preserved remains wrapped in a red cloak with two Dutch coins sewn into his collar. The original marker stone onto which Sanderson inscribed a coded message now sits on the windowsill of Dunsyre kirk.

DUNSYRE – see page 32

DOLPHINTON

Major Learmouth who commanded the Covenanter cavalry at the battle of Rullion Green is buried in the ancient churchyard.

Beechwood tea room   01968 682285

THE ROUTE

	Grid ref.	Miles
1.	111 478	0

Start: Former Dolphinton station by the A702.
Follow the minor road away from the A702 for 200 yards.

| 2. | 111 479 | |

Turn right off minor road, signed right of way to West Linton 4. Continue through gate and then uphill to second gate at White cottage.

| 3. | 112 482 | 1/4 |

Continue through gate and follow track round to left and then towards stand of pine trees. Follow track past Ingraston farm.

| 4. | 135 513 | 2 3/4 |

Eventually you encounter a crossroads. Go straight on passing South Slipperfield cottage to the left, signed – West Linton.

| 5. | 139 513 | 3 1/2 |

Turn left onto golf course road, signed Garvald 3, Dunsyre 5. Follow road through gate at North Slipperfield. Ignore track to the left at sheepfold and continue to small grey building.

| 6. | 123 517 | 4 1/2 |

Continue uphill and turn left, signed – Covenanter's Grave. Follow rough track for 2 miles to four way signpost.

| 7. | 083 515 | 6 1/2 |

Covenanter's Grave is 1/4 mile from the track to your right – follow the line of grouse shooting butts and aim just to the west of the summit.

| 8. | 084 515 | |

A short distance beyond the four-way signpost turn down to the left to follow track – not marked in all maps. Follow through several fords to gate by trees. Continue through gate and follows soft but obvious track through field to Easton Farm.

| 9. | 084 493 | 8 |

Go through awkward gate at farm buildings and go round to the left to take up road downhill. At bottom of the hill turn right and follow road into Dunsyre.

| 10. | 073 482 | 9 |

Turn left in Dunsyre and follow road through piles of old railway bridge. Shortly you encounter a junction where you follow the road to the left, signed – Edinburgh. Continue to follow this road going to the left again at the next junction. Follow road all the way to start point.

| 11 | 111 478 | 12 |

End: former Dolphinton station by the A702. (see map page 46)

Bike Lanarkshire

An original bridge on the Biggar to Edinburgh turnpike.

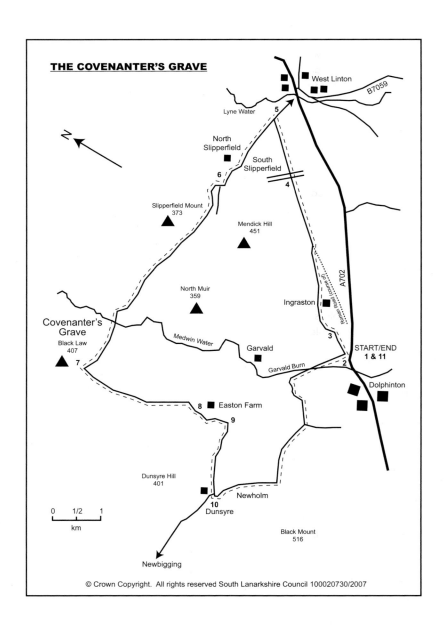

THE COVENANTER'S GRAVE

West Linton

B7059

Lyne Water

5

North
Slipperfield

South
Slipperfield

6

4

Slipperfield Mount
373

Mendick Hill
451

North Muir
359

Ingraston

Roman Road (route of)

A702

Covenanter's
Grave

Black Law
407

7

Medwin Water

Garvald

3

START/END
1 & 11

2

Garvald Burn

Dolphinton

8 Easton Farm

9

Dunsyre Hill
401

10
Dunsyre

Newholm

Black Mount
516

0   1/2   1

km

Newbigging

© Crown Copyright. All rights reserved South Lanarkshire Council 100020730/2007

COULTER AND COWGILL RESERVOIRS

Distance: Coulter village to Coulter reservoir, 4 1/2 miles; Coulter village to Cowgill reservoir, 4 miles.
Grade: easy/moderate
Terrain: it is uphill all the way to both reservoirs is however a very gradual ascent except for a short steep pull just beyond the junction for Nisbet.
Map: OS explorer sheet 336

Getting there: Coulter village straddles the A702 two miles south of Biggar. From the north follow directions for Biggar. From the south leave the M74 at junction 13, Abington and follow signs for Biggar, A702.

BY THE WAY

The trip out to the Coulter and Cowgill reservoirs involves crossing the southern boundary fault, which separates the central lowland from the southern uplands.

The two narrow, steep-sided river valleys that contain the reservoirs penetrate deep into hills that surround Culter Fell (2 445 feet). Out of sight of from the Clyde valley these glens have been settled since the Iron Age and there are abundant remains of forts and settlements on Culter Fell and the small hillocks around Nisbet and Snaip.

The Cowgill reservoir is small and perfectly formed. Surrounded by tall pine trees the reservoirs have a completely natural appearance.

Coulter reservoir is at the head of a wider valley. The dam and the new waterworks are less discrete than at Cowgill but the impression of being at the heart of wild hill country is undiminished.

THE ROUTE

	Grid ref.	Miles
1.	026 338	0

Start: Coulter village hall. Leave park and turn left to T-junction.

2.	025 338	

Turn left at T-junction and cycle away from Coulter village on level road.

3.	028 338	1/2

Follow road to right over bridge and take right fork. Road climbs and then descends to Birthwood.

4.	031 312	2

At Culter Allers road forks. Left for Coulter reservoir and right for Cowgill reservoir.
Coulter reservoir

Coulter reservoir

Following the road round to the left, past entrance to big house and then to the right. Road climbs gently to dam and then steeply to top of dam.

Cowgill reservoirs

Follow level road through trees alongside burn. Road crosses two bridges followed by short stiff climb. Now road climbs steadily across hillside. Road dips to white cottage and then climbs towards the lower Cowgill dam in the trees. Unsurfaced track continues to upper Cowgill reservoir.

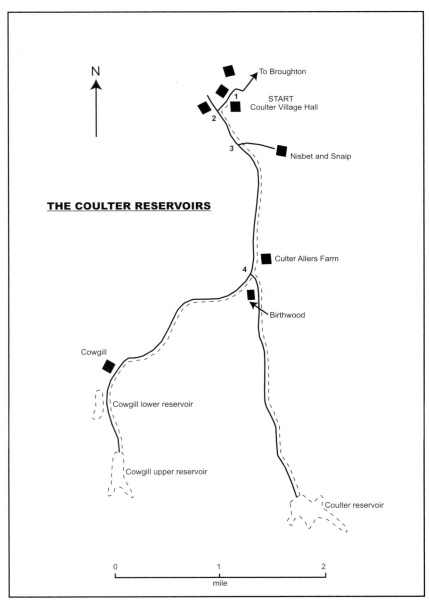

N

To Broughton

START
Coulter Village Hall

1

2

3

Nisbet and Snaip

THE COULTER RESERVOIRS

Culter Allers Farm

4

Birthwood

Cowgill

Cowgill lower reservoir

Cowgill upper reservoir

Coulter reservoir

0   1   2
mile

THE LANARK ROUTES

LANARK

Lanark is an intimate market town that sits high above the Clyde on a classic defensive site, and it can trace its history back to Roman times. Elevated to a Royal Burgh in 1140 by David I, Lanark entered its heyday.

The town was en route for kings wishing to visit the south west of their kingdom or the upper Tweed valley. William I and Alexander II were frequent visitors and Robert the Bruce was patron of a Franciscan friary where the Clydesdale Inn now stands.

It was in 1183 that Pope Lucius II made reference to the town's Lanark Grammar school in a Papal Bull making it one of the oldest schools in Britain.

The claim to fame that Lanark prefers is that William Wallace is reputed to have wooed his wife Marion Braidfute in Lanark, having met her at the town's St Kentigern's church – the ruin of which can be found in the cemetery at the junction of Ladyacre Road and Hyndford Road.

After a street skirmish involving Wallace and some English soldiers garrisoned in Lanark, Edward I's sheriff executed Marion instead of her husband Wallace who had fled the scene.

Wallace avenged her death by killing the sheriff and thus set himself on the path to rebellion against the English occupation and becoming the hero of the Wars of Independence.

A statue of the stocky Wallace is incorporated into the clock tower of St Nicholas church at the foot of the High Street. A plaque opposite marks the likely spot of his Lanark home.

The medieval town was centred on the area around St Nicholas Church. The oldest buildings are marked out by their crow-stepped gables.

The Victorian High Street is nevertheless built on the medieval pattern of burghage plots – long narrow strips of land extending back from the High Street frontage. The building that protrudes at the foot of the High Street is the 18th century tollbooth, which would have served as the town's courtroom and gaol.

NEW LANARK

These days it is New Lanark, Lanark's precocious offspring that gets all the attention. A perfectly preserved 18th century factory village in a stunning woodland setting by the river Clyde it has been designated a World Heritage site by UNESCO. The status was awarded, in part, to recognise the radical programme of social improvement which brought the village to particular prominence.

New Lanark began as a project initiated by Richard Arkwright and David Dale. Arkwright believed that New Lanark would become the Manchester of Scotland and by 1799 four mills were operational, employing 2000 people who were housed in the specially built tenement rows.

Robert Owen took over the running of the mills from his father-in-law David Dale and it was he who enthusiastically pursued a radical programme of social improvement. Not only were the mill workers and their families comparatively well-housed but they were also provided with evening lectures, schooling and nursery care and a co-operative store which was to serve as the prototype for the co-operative movement.

New Lanark went into decline after the mills closed in 1968 and demolition was briefly contemplated but thanks to an enthusiastic housing association and the New Lanark Conservation Trust it is a thriving community and visitor attraction.

Most of the tenements are now occupied: a large part of one tenement row has been converted to an excellent youth hostel, there are the see-it-as-it-was attractions, one of the mills has been converted to a hotel and there are a number of speciality shops.

The Scottish Wildlife Trust has a visitor centre from where they manage the Falls of Clyde nature reserve.

A statue of William Wallace adorns the front of St Nicholas Church

GETTING THERE

ROAD

From Glasgow: leave the M74 at junction 7, Larkhall and follow the A72 – the Clyde valley tourist route – for 12 miles to Lanark. From the south: leave the M74 at junction 12 and then follow the A70 east and left over Hyndford Bridge.

From Edinburgh: leave the M8 at junction 6, Newhouse, signed for Lanark and Airdrie and follow the A73 for 15 miles east via Newmains and Carluke.

Alternatively follow the A70 west out of Edinburgh, signed for Lanark and Ayr, via Juniper Green, Balerno and Carnwath. Beyond carstairs follow the A743 from at Ravenstruther into Lanark.

Journey times: Glasgow/Edinburgh to Lanark 45 minutes to 1 hour.

RAIL

There are two trains an hour between Glasgow and Lanark. Times of arrival and departure differ on a Saturday. On Sundays the service is hourly. Bicycles are conveyed in the passenger areas consequently it is avoid rush hour trains.

EATING AND DRINKING

Lanark (01555 -)

Armando's chip shop & restaurant	90 High Street	663797
The Inn on the Loch	179 Hyndford Road	663638
The Courtyard	3 Castlegate	663900
The Clydesdale Inn	15 Bloomgate	663455
The Crown Tavern	17 Hope Street	664639
Daisies Coffee shop	18 – 22 Broomgate	665209
East India Company	Indian restaurant, 32 Wellgate	663827
Coffee shop	Wide Close	664000
The Horse & Jockey (bar)	56 High Street	662824
The Market Restaurant	Hyndford Road	663658
The Original Tearoom	32 Bannatyne Street	664962
Prego Italian Restaurant	3 High Street	666300
Ristorante La Vigna	40 Wellgate	664320
Valerio's fish and chicken bar	Bannatyne Street	665818
The Wallace Cave Bar	11 Bloomgate	663662
Woodpecker Restaurant & Bar	20 Wide Close	665161

New Lanark

New Lanark Mill Hotel	Mill one	01555 667200

Kirkfieldbank

Kirkfieldbank Tavern	200 Riverside Road	01555 662537

STAYING

Lanark (01555 -)

Cartland Bridge Hotel	Glasgow Road	664426
Bankhead Farm	Braxfield Road	666560
Duneaton	159 Hyndford Road	665487
Jerviswood Mains Farm	Cleghorn Road	663987
The Mains	2 Muir Glen	660219
St Catherine's B&B	1 Kenilworth Road	662295
Summerlea	32 Hyndford Road	664889

New Lanark (01555 -)

New Lanark Mill hotel	Mill one	667200
New Lanark Youth Hostel (SYHA)	Wee Row, Rosedale Street	666710

Kirkfieldbank (01555 -)

Brig End B&B	231 Riverside Road	663855
Corehouse Farm		661377
Clarkston Farm		663751
Clyde valley caravan park		663951

Outdoor equipment and cycle spares

Frasers of Lanark	2 Bannatyne Street, Lanark	01555 665606
Halfords	Unit 6B Braidfute retail park, Lanark	01555 678410

LANARK, TINTO AND COVINGTON

Tinto hill's graceful cone dominates the skyline throughout Lanarkshire. It is a special place for Lanarkshire people who mark important dates such as the New Year with a climb to it summit. Tinto is the primary goal of this route that has a little bit of everything that is best about cycling in rural Lanarkshire. The route follows mainly quiet roads however there is one mile on the A70 between Carstairs and Ravenstruther.

Distance: 25 miles
Grade: moderate
Terrain: it is only when crossing from one river valley to another that you have to part with some puff and even then not for long. The climb out of Kirkfieldbank, early in the route, is challenging in places. There are several moderate inclines throughout the route but none is especially sustained.
Map: OS Landranger sheet 72

BY THE WAY

KIRKFIELDBANK

A steep descent from Lanark takes you into Kirkfieldbank. From the relatively new bridge over the river Clyde you can take in the 17th century Clydesholm bridge. The narrow stone bridge was the only means of crossing the Clyde until 1959.

THE BONNINGTON LINN

The furthest upstream of the series of four waterfalls known as the Falls of Clyde can be reached by following the road indicated as a dead end just before the turning for Sandilands - distance 1 mile one-way.

The Linn is a complex cataract and is perhaps the most intimidating of the Falls of Clyde. Rocks jut out and the water surges through narrow channels accentuating its power. The best place to view the falls is from the left bank just a short walk from the weir.

THE DOUGLAS VALLEY

The cyclist is treated to peaceful lanes lined with hedgerows and stone dykes and a classic rural landscape of patchwork fields and mature trees. Pause on the humped backed bridge over the Douglas Water to survey the scene.

CARMICHAEL (see also Carmichael circular route)

Rolling up to the crossroads in Carmichael an old signpost points in every direction but the one you want to take. Straight on is the family home and estate of the chief of the clan Carmichael, as is the main entrance to Carmichael church.

The clan Carmichael has occupied these lands for almost 1000 years and the current chief can boast some illustrious forebears. The 2nd Lord Carmichael was a commissioner for the treaty of union and the 3rd a statesman and ambassador to Prussia, Russia and Vienna who negotiated the peace at Aix-la-Chapelle. A memorial to his memory stands on Carmichael hill.

There has been a church in Carmichael dedicated to St Michael since the 12th century. The current church was built in 1750 however an external staircase from original pre-reformation church has been incorporated.

The small park by the church is a pleasant spot for a picnic lunch.

TINTO HILL AND THE TEAROOM
The road from Carmichael to the Tinto tearoom is an engrossing cycle. It twists and turns and you always seem to have enough momentum to reach the top of the next crest. The road cuts across Tinto's heathery north flanks and the views into the corries can be impressive.

Tinto has been a special place for the people of Lanarkshire for several millennia. There are many prehistoric sites on and around the hill and at the summit is Scotland's largest cairn. The cairn was built during the Bronze Age probably as a burial site although it may also have been used for fixing the date of the winter solstice.

At 707 metres it is the highest point in the Central Lowlands however it is not the highest point in Lanarkshire as was once thought. The old rhyme "Twixt Tintock Tap and Culter Fell there is just the third part of an ell" (Scot's Ell = 15 in.) was often repeated until it was established that Culter Fell, five miles to the south-east, was over 100 feet higher.

As result everyone who climbs Tinto is encouraged to carry a stone to the top and add it to the huge cairn. At the present rate of growth it will be 3,500 years before it reaches 2456 feet, one foot higher than Culter Fell.

The climb to the top follows an obvious path and takes one to one-and-a-half hours. The hill's isolated position makes it a terrific viewpoint.

The tearoom is about 100 yards beyond the walkers' car park. It was opened in 1938 at the height of the boom in outdoor pursuits.

DONALD CARGILL MEMORIAL
A welcome free wheel takes you through Thankerton but not quite over the main railway line. About 1/2 mile out of the village on the uphill just beyond Covington Mill there is a memorial on the left hand side to Donald Cargill.

Cargill, a hardline Covenanter, who along with Richard Cameron denounced King Charles II in the Declaration of Sanquhar of 1680 had, as result, a bounty of 500 merks placed on his head. Cargill who had just returned from preaching in the field at Dunsyre was arrested nearby in July 1681 by Irvine of Bonshawe, a bounty hunter. Soon afterwards Cargill was executed in Edinburgh.

COVINGTON

The road continues to climb gently to Newtown of Covington with its thatched cottages. Beyond the hamlet lies a remarkable collection of buildings at Covington.

The tower, built by an infamous branch of the Lindsay family, and the church date from the 15th century. The walls of the tower are 11 feet thick and surrounded by a dry moat. Within the walls there is a pit dungeon and a garderobe (toilet).

The church, which is no longer in use, occupies a site that has been used for religious worship for over 1000 years. A wander in the churchyard provides an interesting insight into life through the ages here.

At the entrance to the farm is a well-preserved beehive style dovecot built in the 16th century. It would have housed 500 pigeons and provided a regular supply of eggs and fresh meat.

On the opposite side of the road there is a cairn that commemorates the night spent here by Robert Burns on his way to Edinburgh in 1786.

PETTINAIN (alternative route)

It is a short sharp incline into pretty hamlet of Pettinain. Stone flints discovered in the area suggest that this prominent hillock has been occupied by since 6,500 BC. It is also an ancient religious site and records show that there was a priest here in 1147. The current church, no longer in use, was built in the 17th century.

CARSTAIRS JUNCTION AND CARSTAIRS VILLAGE

It is possible to end the route early at Carstairs Junction and return by train to Glasgow and Edinburgh but not Lanark. The trains are infrequent and you should check timetables before setting out. No Sunday service.

Carstairs village is a pleasant place arranged a village green. The church overlooking the green dates from the 17th century and has ancient communion ware on display.

| **The Green Granary** | 16 Carstairs Road | 01555 871202 |
| **The Village Inn** | 89 Lanark Road | 01555 870214 |

THE ROUTE

	Grid ref.	Miles
1.	**886 436**	**0**

Start: Lanark railway station. Leave the station car park and turn right. Go straight through at traffic lights and follow High Street downhill. Go through narrow gap at foot of High Street. Continue downhill.

| **2.** | **875 438** | **1/2** |

Turn left onto the A72 – signed Hamilton 13 & Clyde Valley Tourist Route. Descend steep and twisty road and cross Clyde.

| **3.** | **868 437** | **3/4** |

Take first left on far side of bridge. Climb uphill for 400 yards.

| **4.** | **869 435** | **1** |

Turn left off Riverside Road at fork at flats. Climb for 1 mile – steep in places.

| **5.** | **875 418** | **2** |

Surfaced road turns sharply to right. Follow to T-junction.

| **6.** | **874 416** | **2 1/4** |

Turn left onto gently descending road and follow for 2 miles

| **7.** | **884 394** | **4** |

Follow road round to right in trees. Take next left – signed Sandilands 1 3/4. Restrain speed on fast downhill as road takes sharp right over bridge at foot of hill.

| **8.** | **892 386** | **5 1/2** |

At T-junction beyond milk tanker depot turn right and follow road round to left. Climb to junction with A70.

| **9.** | **895 379** | **5 3/4** |

Turn left onto cycle path by A70 and then at its end cross the A70 for quiet road – signed Carmichael 2. Follow road to junction at farm.

| **10.** | **905 380** | **6** |

Turn right and follow road to crossroads.

| **11.** | **921 384** | **7 3/4** |

Old signpost at crossroads. Turn right – unsigned. Continue through Carmichael.

| **12.** | **926 380** | **8** |

Road ahead is very steep, however turn right at foot of hill.

| **13.** | **924 364** | **9** |

Follow road round to left where dead end in indicated straight ahead. Follow road through Lochlyvoch farm and the round the foot of Tinto Hill to A73.

| **14.** | **966 378** | **12** |

Go straight on at A73 – signed Thankerton.

| **15.** | **973 378** | **12 1/2** |

Just beyond bowling club turn left onto Boat Road – signed Carstairs 6, Carnwath 7. Follow road over railway line and continue straight on at next junction and then uphill past Cargill memorial on left.

| **16.** | **972 405** | **15** |

1/2 mile beyond Covington Tower follow road round to the left and then turn right – signed Pettinain and cycleway. Follow road to junction.

17.   **961 426**   **16 1/2**

Turn right and after 1/2 mile follow road to the left at Grangehall. Beyond Grangehall climb moderately and then descend steeply in cutting. Follow road over Clyde into Carstairs Junction to T-junction at church.

18.   **955 451**   **18 1/2**

Turn left and then and follow road uphill to cross railway bridge. Follow road into Carstairs Village.

19.   **937 460**   **20**

At village green continue to junction with A70. Turn left onto A70 and follow out of Carstairs.

20.   **921 451**   **21**

In Ravenstruther take right turn onto quiet road and follow into Cleghorn. Continue through village to traffic lights.

21.   **905 452**   **22**

Turn left at traffic lights and follow A706 into Lanark.

22.   **881 440**   **23 3/4**

Turn left beyond fire station and then take second right. At foot of hill turn left and go uphill. Dismount at top of hill and push bike through to High Street.

23.   **884 436**   **24**

Return to station on Bannatyne Street (right fork).

24.   **886 436**   **24**

End: Lanark railway station (see map page 58)

Old signpost Carmichael

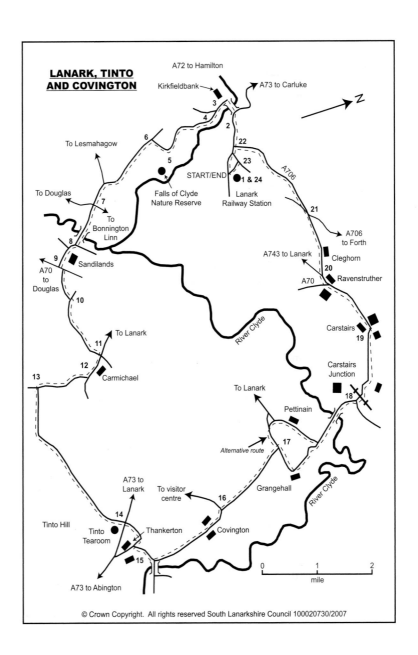

LANARK, TINTO AND COVINGTON

A72 to Hamilton

A73 to Carluke

Kirkfieldbank

N

3

4

2

To Lesmahagow

6

22

23

5

START/END

1 & 24

A706

Lanark Railway Station

Falls of Clyde Nature Reserve

To Douglas

7

To Bonnington Linn

21

A706 to Forth

8

A743 to Lanark

Cleghorn

9

Sandilands

20

Ravenstruther

A70 to Douglas

A70

10

River Clyde

Carstairs

19

To Lanark

11

Carstairs Junction

12

18

13

Carmichael

To Lanark

Pettinain

Alternative route

17

To Lanark

Grangehall

River Clyde

A73 to Lanark

To visitor centre

16

Tinto Hill

14

Thankerton

Covington

Tinto Tearoom

15

A73 to Abington

0   1   2
        mile

© Crown Copyright. All rights reserved South Lanarkshire Council 100020730/2007

CARMICHAEL CIRCULAR

This is a gem of a route. Although relatively short it includes the best and quietest sections of the Lanark and Tinto tour. It also includes a section through the historic Carmichael estate.

Distance: 9 miles or 11 miles
Grade: easy/moderate
Terrain: in terms of hills the longer route is more gradual. The steepest hill is just beyond the Eagle gates at the entrance to Carmichael estate – it is however short. The road surface is generally good however the first few hundred yards is rough and the driveway through the estate can also be rough in places.

BY THE WAY

CARMICHAEL VISITOR CENTRE

The visitor centre includes a waxwork museum, children's play park, a shop from where you can buy high quality venison farmed on the Carmichael estate and a restaurant.

CARMICHAEL ESTATE

You enter the estate through the eagle gates. These Silesia eagles are a tribute to the efforts of the 2nd earl of Hyndford in negotiating the peace between Silesia and Prussia. He was ambassador to Vienna and Russia and a commissioner of the Treaty of Union of 1701.

This has been the Carmichael clan's patch since the 14th century. The nearby hamlet and family take their name from a church founded by Queen Margaret in 1058 and dedicated to St Michael.

The church was built on Kirk Hill, which is on your left as you cycle along the estate drive.

Not much further on, and a short walk off the drive, is the old Carmichael House. Built in stages from 1734 by 3rd earl of Hyndford it replaced a fortified tower destroyed by Cromwell. The covered corridor that linked both wings and was added later relieved the need to have a horse and carriage standing by, ready to transport the earl between two. The house has fallen into ruin since its roof was removed in 1952.

At Westmains there is a very dovecot built c. 1750 which stands 20 metres and is reckoned to be one of the best examples in Scotland.

CARMICHAEL, see page 53

TINTO HILL, see page 54

COVINGTON, see page 55

THE ROUTE

	Grid ref.	Miles
1.	948 389	0

Start: Carmichael visitor centre, Warrenhill.

Leave car park and take care crossing the A73 and take rough road, just over to the left, uphill to junction.

2.	949 395	1/4

Turn left at junction. Follow road down to the left to return to A73. Once again take care crossing the A73 and continue through the Eagle gates and uphill on the estate drive. Follow drive around the walled garden by going to the right then left and the follow drive all the way to West gate.

3.	925 386	2 1/4

Leave estate by West gate and continue to crossroads indicated by old signpost. Turn to the left – unsigned and continue through Carmichael village. When road starts to climb steeply turn right.

4.	924 365	4

Follow to the left through Locklyvoch farm when straight ahead is indicated as dead end. Beyond Lochlyvoch farm follow road round Tinto to junction with A73.

5.	965 378	7

Cross A73 and follow road downhill into Fallburn. (Shorter route follows Perryflats Road to the left before play park, turn left a T-junction and resume route from 8). For longer route continue into Thankerton.

6.	973 379	7 1/2

Just beyond bowling club turn left onto Boat Road – signed Carstairs 6, Carnwath 7. Follow road over railway line and continue straight on at next junction and then uphill past Cargill memorial on left.

7.	971 405	9 1/2

1/2 mile beyond Covington Tower follow road round to the left and then continue past the turning for Pettinain onto Meadowflats Road.

8.	949 395	11

Take second left at trees. Descend rough road to A73 and cross to visitor centre.

9.	948 389	11 1/4

End: Carmichael visitor centre

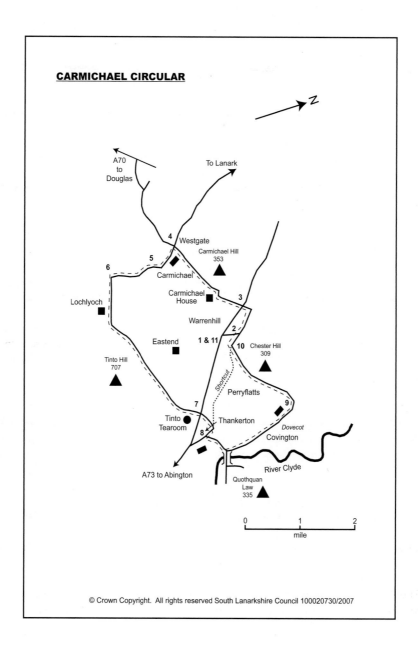

CARMICHAEL CIRCULAR

N

A70
to
Douglas

To Lanark

4 Westgate

Carmichael Hill
353

5

6

Carmichael

Carmichael
House

3

Lochlyoch

Warrenhill

2

Eastend

1 & 11

10 Chester Hill
309

Tinto Hill
707

Shortcut

Perryflatts

7

9

Tinto
Tearoom

Thankerton

8

Dovecot
Covington

A73 to Abington

River Clyde

Quothquan
Law
335

0   1   2

mile

THE FOUR VALLEYS

A route that takes in four valleys can only mean lots of ups and downs. It offers an entirely different perspective on the Clyde and its tributary valleys. From the high ground you can appreciate the surprising depth of the valley and take in the stunning view of the Southern Highlands.

In each valley you will discover a hidden world of quiet lanes that wind between smallholdings, old farms and orchards.

To reach Craignethan Castle is a very challenging cycle however this unique fastness is the highlight of the tour.

Distance: 18 miles
Grade: very hard
Terrain: this is a route for fit cyclists. Each valley involves a steep climb and a steep descent. Some of the downhill sections require restraint.
Map: OS Landranger sheet 72

BY THE WAY

CARTLAND BRIDGE

The long descent pauses briefly, as should you, on Cartland Bridge. Designed by Thomas Telford it spans the Mouse (moose), in three arches, 125 feet below.

Legend has it that Wallace hid in a cave in the side of the gorge – it is not advisable to attempt to find it.

The impressive gate house at the bottom of the hill is part of the Lee Castle estate.

NEMPHLAR

Nemphlar, a former weaving hamlet, sits on a high spur of land that separates the Lee valley from that of the Clyde. The views are impressive in all directions and be sure to look back towards Lanark and Tinto hill.

CROSSFORD

A steep and increasingly twisty descent brings you to Crossford. Near the bottom look out for the red roof tiles visible through the trees as this is your cue to put the brakes on.
Despite the name there is no need to get your feet wet crossing the Clyde. Instead you enter the village on the fine 18th century sandstone bridge.

The Clyde valley's fruit growing industry is centred on Crossford and there are plenty of garden centres with coffee shops and opportunities to pick strawberries.

Fruit has been grown in the Clyde valley since Roman times. Merlin sang about the orchards of the Clyde in the 6th century and the Venerable Bede refers to them in an eighth century verse.

Tillietudlem Inn	14 Lanark Road	01555 860555
The Riverside Coffee House	Valley International Park	01555 861189

TILLIETUDLEM AND CRAIGNETHAN CASTLE

Craignethan Castle may or may not have provided Sir Walter Scott with the inspiration for Tillietudlem Castle which features in his book Old Mortality but the link has grown so strong that the hamlet closest to the castle has adopted the name Tillietudlem and the castle.

At first sight across the river Nethan the castle seems to have been built in the perfect position as it is surrounded on three sides by a steep ravine. But as you cycle along the drive towards the castle its fatal weakness becomes apparent – the ground on the remaining side is higher and from there, there is an excellent view of inside the curtain wall. The castle was therefore particularly vulnerable to attack by artillery.

Begun in 1530 by James Hamilton of Finnart, it was the last private fortress to be built in Scotland.

A distinctive feature of its defences, and unique in Britain, is the castle's caponier. Situated at the bottom of the ditch that defends the weak west side the idea was that the ditch could be scoured by hand gunners secure in this vaulted chamber.

The castle was captured and recaptured several times in a 50 year period of military activity and every time without a fight. The castle attracted this attention because of Hamilton's support for Mary Queen of Scots after her abdication in 1567 and she is known to have sheltered here in May 1568.

With its imposing towers, ruined ramparts and a deep ditch there is enough of Craignethan Castle left to take up an hour of your time. More information at: www.historic-scotland.gov.uk

BLACKHILL (National Trust for Scotland)

Beyond Auchenheath the route returns to delightfully peaceful lanes. The sting in the tail is however another climb over the shoulder of Blackhill. At the top of the climb a footpath leads off to the summit of the hill (15 minutes). The informal trust site is the summit of the hill where the remains of an Iron Age fort and a later settlement still clearly visible. There are expansive views in every direction.

THE ROUTE

	Grid ref.	Miles
1.	886 436	0

Start: Lanark railway station. Leave the station car park and turn right. Go straight through at traffic lights and follow High Street downhill. Go through narrow gap at foot of High Street. Continue downhill out of Lanark past entrance to Cartland Bridge Hotel.

2.	868 445	1 3/4

Turn left immediately after crossing Cartland bridge. Take the right hand fork signed, Nemphlar 1. Descend past Lee Castle lodge and then climb moderately along narrow road to Nemphlar.

3.	856 449	2 1/4

At old signpost turn right for Crossford. After short climb a long straight downhill opens up. Road then turns steeply downhill. Prepare to stop at T-junction when you spot red roof tiles.

4.	831 466	4 1/4

At T-junction turn left and cross bridge into Crossford.

5.	827 465	4 1/2

Beyond bridge turn right onto A72. Cycle through village.

6.	824 469	5

At the Tillietudlem Inn turn left steeply uphill, signed – Craignethan Castle.

7.	822 459	5 1/2

At top of hill just beyond row of houses turn right signed – Craignethan Castle 1. Road descends very steeply (12%) and bottoms out at Corra Mill. Road is level for short distance and then climbs just as steeply to Tillietudlem in a series of hairpin bends.

8.	792 430	9 1/2

At the end of Southfield Road turn left onto Carlisle Road.

9.	799 430	10

Follow Carlisle Road to the junction at Kirkmuirhill Parish Church. Turn left signed – Lanark 6, Craignethan Castle 4, Auchenheath 1. Follow road downhill over narrow bridge and then uphill into Auchenheath.

10.	809 437	11

At crossroads in Auchenheath turn right onto Newkays Road.

11.	823 431	12

Follow road downhill and straight through at crossroads. Road dips and then climbs steeply to Stonebyres reservoir. Descend to T-junction with B7018.

12.	838 432	13

Turn left onto B7018 and follow downhill through trees.

13.	852 431	13 3/4

Take the next right – a narrow road and unsigned. Follow rising road past cottages to T-junction.

14.	867 430	15

Turn left and descend into Kirkfieldbank to emerge at junction in village. Turn right and cross bridge over Clyde.

15. **868 440** **15 3/4**

Once over Clyde take first left and continue past campsite and then steeply uphill turning left to arrive at T-junction with A73.

16. **868 445** **16 1/4**

Turn right over Cartland Bridge and retrace outward route into Lanark (broad pavement available).

17. **886 436** **18**

End: Lanark railway station. (see map page 66)

Craignethan Castle

THE FOUR VALLEYS

1 & 17
START/END

Lanark Railway Station

2 & 16

A73 to Carluke

Kirkfieldbank

3

15

Nemphlar

14

4
Crawford

A72 to Hamilton

6

5 Crossford

13

7

Craignethan Castle

12

Tillietudlem

11

10

Auchenheath

8 **9**

B7078 to Larkhall

B7078 to Lesmahagow

Blackwood Kirkmuirhill

0   1   2
mile

© Crown Copyright. All rights reserved South Lanarkshire Council 100020730/2007

LANARK ROBERTON AND DOUGLAS

This route links two of Lanarkshire's oldest and most historic burghs. At first the route bumps along the Douglas valley before climbing over the shoulder of Tinto hill and then over the pass between Dungavel Hill and Roberton Law to Roberton. From the most southerly point the route hooks north via Douglas and the opposite side of the Douglas valley.

Distance: 36 1/2 miles
Grade: hard
Terrain: Two high passes follow in quick succession. The first is more demanding than the second climbing in stages through 500 feet from the floor of the Douglas valley in under three miles. There are several other moderate to steep climbs however all are relatively short.
Map: OS Landranger sheet 72

BY THE WAY

Large villas, the livestock auction market, the old racecourse and the Winston barracks line the road. Each reflects an aspect of Lanark's once illustrious past as a county town, market town and important garrison town – all but the auction mart is now defunct.

HYNDFORD BRIDGE

This fine old sandstone bridge was built in 1773 and it is still the only way to cross the Clyde at this point.

GARF WATER VALLEY

The Garf water curves around Tinto hill's hidden and much less visited southern side. The view from the high point of the road (1100 feet) is magnificent taking in Tinto, Culter Fell and the Lowther Hills. Hang gliders and parapenters are a common sight as are birds of prey.

ROBERTON

The top of pass between Dungavel Hill and Roberton Law also offers terrific views. It is however a much gentler ascent. The descent into Roberton is, however, eye-watering. The hillsides are unfenced and sheep regularly wander into road.

The hamlet of Roberton is an ancient settlement. The houses cling to steep slopes along the Roberton burn, which is spanned by a 17th century bridge.

DOUGLAS

The northward route follows a cycle path across the Red Moss a large exposed area of moor before descending to the A70 two miles east of Douglas.

The route follows the cycle path east but it is well worth making the detour into Douglas.

Douglas takes its name from the family who in the 13th and 14th centuries were among the most powerful in Scotland and controlled most of the south-west. Douglas was the family powerbase and consequently Douglas has a rich history that can be immediately appreciated by wandering its narrow streets.

On Main Street there is a memorial cairn to James Gavin, a tailor and covenanter who had his ears cut off with his own shears by Bloody Claverhouse and then banished to Barbados. The lintel he carved is incorporated into the memorial.

At the centre of the village, with its 15th century octagonal tower is St Bride's Church. The clock in the tower is reckoned to be the oldest working clock in Scotland and was presented to the church in 1565 by Mary queen of Scots. In the spirit of the Douglas family motto 'Never behind' it chimes three minutes before the hour.

A sign on the gate to the churchyard will tell you were you can obtain the key to the church and once inside you can peer through the glass set in the floor at the casket containing the heart of The Good Sir James Douglas who was Robert the Bruce's right hand man in the fight with England; the other casket contains the heart of Sir Archibald Douglas who died in 1513.

Sir James promised the dying Bruce that he would take his heart to the Holy Land so that in some way Bruce's desire to fight in a crusade could be fulfilled. Sir James was killed in Spain fighting the Moors, en route to the Holy Land. His time worn tomb and those of other Douglasses are set against the walls. A beautifully carved and slightly spooky marble effigy of Lucy Elizabeth, countess of Home sits on the altar.

Not far from St Bride's is the pointing statue of the Earl of Angus. He is pointing to the field in which the Angus regiment later known as the Cameronians was raised in 1689. The Cameronians take their name from Richard Cameron, a hard line and prominent Covenanter who was behind the treasonable declaration of Sanquhar of 1680. Cameron was killed in a skirmish with dragoons at Aird's Moss in Ayrhsire.

It was in the building across the narrow road from St Bride's , which was once the Sun Inn and at the time of the Covenanters the tollbooth, that Bloody Claverhouse rested after Aird's Moss with the severed head and hands of Richard Cameron. The Sun Inn, built in 1621, is Douglas's oldest intact building and is now a private residence.

Countryside Inn	Main Street	01555 851218
Douglas Arms hotel	52 Ayr Road	01555 851322
Cross Keys	68 Main Street	01555 851435
Spice of Life	15 Main Street	01555 850200
The Frying Scotsman	56 Ayr Road	01555 851043
Cairn Lodge Services	Happendon	01555 851880

BROKEN CROSS MUIR

The final leg of the return route skirts Broken Muir and it is close to here that Donald McDonald aide de camp to Bonnie Prince Charlie was arrested by a Whig mob. He was then taken to Carlisle where he was executed.

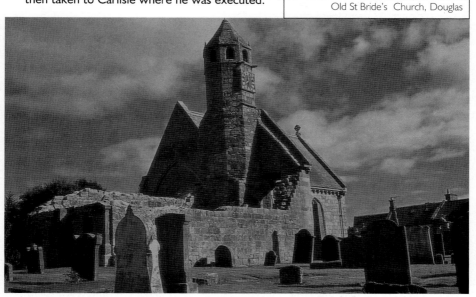

Old St Bride's Church, Douglas

THE ROUTE - Lanark to Douglas

	Grid ref.	Miles
1.	886 436	0

Start: Lanark railway station. Leave station and turn left. Proceed to roundabout.

2.   887 433   1/4

Take the second exit signed – Carlisle, A73. Follow Hyndford Road out of Lanark. Descend to traffic lights at Hyndford bridge.

3.   914 414   2

Cross bridge and turn right signed – Ayr, A70. Follow A70 for 1 mile.

4.   904 400   3

Just as A70 narrows to single lane turn right onto narrow lane. Continue to Sandilands and follow road round to left.

5.   892 384   4 1/2

Turn right at red telephone box. Road climbs gently at first to T-junction opposite low cottage.

6.   881 358   6 1/2

Turn left and cycle short distance to crossroads with A70.

7.   885 354   6 3/4

Go straight over at A70, signed B7055, Wiston 5 1/2. Follow road uphill. Fast downhill into Garf valley follows. Prepare to turn right at cottage.

8.   **925 331**   **9 1/2**

Turn right at white cottage, signed – Roberton 3. Climb steadily over pass. Very fast descent into Roberton. Cattle grids and free roaming sheep are a hazard. Cycle through Roberton to junction with A73.

9.   **946 286**   **12 3/4**

Turn right onto A73 and follow for 1 1/2 miles.

10.   **935 262**   **14 1/4**

Just beyond roundabout turn right. Climb moderately to B7078 and cycle-path.

11.   **901 253**   **16 1/2**

Cross B7078 and join cycle-path. Long crossing of exposed Red Moss follows. Cycle path become cycle lane and descends to junction with A70.

12.   **855 326**   **22**

Turn left and follow A70 for 2 miles into Douglas. Turn right for return route to Lanark and follow from point 14 below.

13.   **835 309**   **24**

From old St Bride's Church go away from the village centre and follow the Colonel's Entry and follow uphill to junction with A70. Turn left onto A70.

Douglas to Lanark

14.   **856 327**   **26**

Go straight through first roundabout, signed – Lanark, Coalburn services.

15.   **859 330**

At second roundabout turn left, signed - Glasgow B7078.

16.   **855 334**   **26 1/2**

500 yards from roundabout turn right through gap in central reservation onto minor road, signed Douglas Water 3. Short climb followed by gently undulating road. Follow road to T-junction.

17.   **867 364**   **30 1/2**

Turn right and follow this road all the way to Kirkfieldbank (ignore all side roads). Follow road round to the right at Newhouse Farm for downhill into Kirkfieldbank.

18.   **868 439**   **35**

At bottom of hill at T-junction with A72 turn right and cross bridge.

19.   **868 440**

Once over Clyde take first left and continue past campsite and then steeply uphill turning left to arrive at T-junction with A73.

20.   **868 445**   **35 1/2**

Turn right onto A73 and follow into Lanark (broad pavement available). Continue uphill into the centre of Lanark to traffic light at the top of High Street.

21.   **884 436**   **36 1/2**

Take right fork for Bannatyne St and cycle short distance to Lanark railway station.

22.   **886 436**   **36 1/2**

End: Lanark railway station.

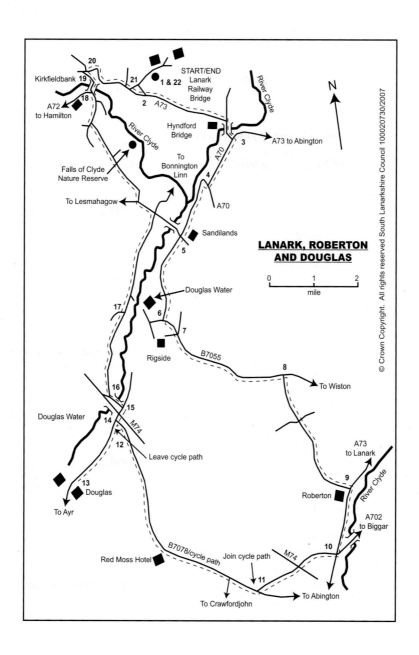

Kirkfieldbank **19**
20
21
1 & 22 START/END
Lanark Railway Bridge
18
A72 to Hamilton
2 A73
River Clyde
River Clyde
N
Hyndford Bridge
A73 to Abington
Falls of Clyde Nature Reserve
To Bonnington Linn
3
A70
To Lesmahagow
4
A70
Sandilands
5

LANARK, ROBERTON AND DOUGLAS

Douglas Water
17
6
7
Rigside
B7055
8
To Wiston

0   1   2
mile

16
Douglas Water
15
14
M74
A73 to Lanark
12
Leave cycle path
9
Roberton
River Clyde
13
Douglas
A702 to Biggar
To Ayr
B7078/cycle path
Join cycle path
M74
10
Red Moss Hotel
11
To Crawfordjohn
To Abington

NUTBERRY HILL (off-road)

This route explores the forestry that covers the low hills to the west of Douglas. The road eventually emerges from the trees to loop around the summit of Nutberry Hill (532 m) from where there are excellent views in every direction.

To the north the whole of the central Scotland lies before you and the view extends beyond the Campsie Fells to Ben Lomond and the southern highlands.

Distance: 16 miles
Grade: hard
Terrain: there are many short stiff climbs and free flowing descents between Douglas West and the summit of Nutberry Hill. For the most part the surface is very good but there are some soft sections and mossy stretches which can be greasy

The final thrilling descent falls plummets through 100 metres in just half a mile.

Map: OS Explorer sheet 335

Getting there: from the M74 follow the A70 through Douglas and take the first right just beyond the village, signed for Douglas West. Follow all the way to the road end.

THE ROUTE

	Grid ref.	Miles
1.	821 310	0

Start: Douglas West. Go through gate to take up rough road that climbs towards the Scottish Power wind farm on Hagshaw Hill.

2.	811 317	2/3

At fork in the road go off to the right into the forestry.
Follow the forestry road for about five miles ignoring all side roads. It is often necessary to consult the map in order to be sure of the way forward.

3.	744 330	6 1/2

Clockwise around Nutberry Hill starts with a steep climb followed by a long level section and long free flowing descent which can be greasy in places. Return to Douglas West by outward route.

4.	821 310	16

End: Douglas West

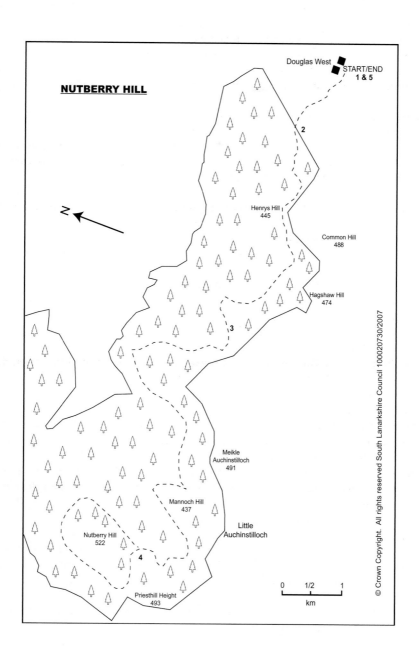

NUTBERRY HILL

Douglas West

START/END
1 & 5

2

Henrys Hill
445

Common Hill
488

Hagshaw Hill
474

3

Meikle
Auchinstilloch
491

Mannoch Hill
437

Little
Auchinstilloch

Nutberry Hill
522

4

Priesthill Height
493

0   1/2   1

km

FORTH, WILSONTOWN, AUCHENGRAY AND BRAEHEAD

This often forgotten corner of Lanarkshire was at the vanguard of the industrial revolution. Mining and railway paraphernalia is to be found along the way as is the Wilsontown ironworks one of the first in Scotland and now a national monument. Industry has been important but Forth is surrounded by very pleasant countryside.

Distance: 15 miles
Grade: moderate
Terrain: A short climb to Auchengray and there is a climb past Ampherlaw House however neither climb is particularly difficult. Mostly the route is pleasantly undulating.
Map: OS Landranger sheet 72

GETTING THERE
ROAD
From the south: leave M74 at junction 12 and follow A70 to Lanark. From Lanark follow the A706 east – take first right beyond foot of High St, signed - Forth and Linlithgow.
From north and west: leave M8 at junction 6 and follow A73, signed Lanark and Peebles. At Carluke follow the A721 for Peebles and after 5 miles turn left at the Harelaw roundabout to take up the A706 for Forth.

From the east: follow the A71 out of Edinburgh follow either the A704 or A706 from West Calder.

RAIL
Nearest stations: Lanark 8 miles; Shotts(Dykehead) 6 miles.

BY THE WAY
WILSONTOWN
Not more than a mile from Forth is Wilsontown a community that grew up around the ironworks founded here in 1779 by the Wilson brothers. Locally available coal, limestone and ironstone made it the perfect location for an ironworks.

These were the first ironworks in Lanarkshire and only the second in Scotland. So successful were the works that by 1812 over 2000 people lived in the village. A church, a school and a bakery were built in this otherwise empty landscape.

1812 was however the beginning of the end for Wilsontown as the spiralling costs of transportation and squabbling among the brothers brought litigation and bankruptcy. The works were rarely in service after 1812 and were closed in 1824.

The Forestry Commission has developed a series of walks that explore the ironworks site and the adjoining woodland.

HAYWOOD

Haywood is barely recognisable today as a settlement but it was once a mining village of 1200 inhabitants and had all the amenities of a thriving community including a railway station.

The ruin overlooking Haywood was once a hotel. On the windowsill there is a carved lament to the desolation, addressed to Annie a former landlady:

O Annie wert thou here tae see, A waefu (woeful) wummin thou wad be.

AUCHENGRAY

After probably the most significant climb of the route you encounter the small rural community of Auchengray. A once thriving rural community, the row of houses around the small square housed an undertaker, a post office, a pub and a smithy. The Auchengray Inn survived until recently but is now a private home.

The village church is particularly distinctive. The facade facing the road was designed by modern gothic architect FT Pilkington in the style of a Coptic church in Alexandria, Egypt.

BRAEHEAD

Cameronian minister John MacMillan established a church between 1743 and 1753.

The Last Shift Inn　　　Carnwath Road　　　01555 812700

THE ROUTE

	Grid ref.	Miles
1.	942 538	0

Start: Forth Kirk, Main Street.

With your back to the church go to the left. After 50 yards turn left onto Manse Road. Follow road past bowling club and recreation ground. Eventually arrive at fork in the road at disused church.

2.	949 546	1

Take left fork then next right, signed – Haywood 2, Auchengray 4.

3.	948 548	1 1/4

Almost immediately turn right again and enter Wilsontown. Follow road round to the left out of Wilsontown. Road dog legs at Haywood. Follow the road over the level crossing and then uphill to T-junction at Auchengray.

4.	996 543	5

Turn right into Auchengray. Continue through Auchengray. On downhill go to the left when road swings to right. Follow undulating road.

5.	994 503	7 1/2

Take right, after Pat Baxter furnishing, through a small group of houses in the trees. Climb past the entrance to Ampherlaw House.

6.	987 511	8

Follow road round to the left over railway bridge. Continue over sandstone bridge and then uphill to T-junction.

7.	973 516	9

Turn left. Follow road to junction overlooked by Eastshields Tower.

8.	959 501	10 1/4

Turn left then right at crossroads. Follow road for about 1 mile. Take right opposite Scabgill Farm. Follow road into Braehead and proceed along Main Street to T-junction opposite Last Shift Inn.

9.	955 508	11 1/4

Turn left. Leave Braehead on the downhill. Continue along this road following signs for Wilsontown B7016. Eventually arrive at cemetery and disused church. Turn left at church and return into Forth on Manse Road.

10.	942 538	14 1/2

End: Forth Kirk, Main Street.

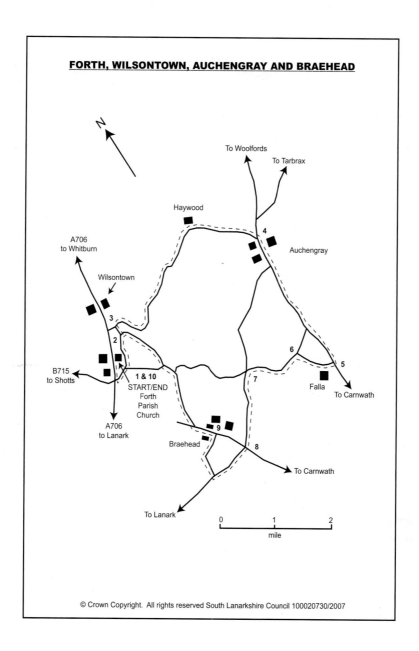

FORTH, WILSONTOWN, AUCHENGRAY AND BRAEHEAD

To Woolfords

To Tarbrax

Haywood

A706
to Whitburn

4

Auchengray

Wilsontown

3

2

B715
to Shotts

1 & 10
START/END
Forth
Parish
Church

6

5

7

Falla

To Carnwath

A706
to Lanar

9

8

Braehead

To Carnwath

To Lanark

0   1   2
mile

LANARK, YIELDSHIELDS, CARTLAND AND KILNCADZOW

This is a good route to fill a spare morning or afternoon. It takes advantage of the quiet back roads that cross the high moor to the north of Lanark. The cycling is pleasant and varied. There are good views and an exceptional bakery at Kilncadzow.

Elsewhere views can also be exceptional. From the Harelaw roundabout you can take in the Pentlands, the Broughton Heights and Culter Fell stretching across the southern horizon from east to west.

From the high point between Kilncadzow and Yieldshields, over 1000 feet the view is to the west and north. It is easy to pick out Ben Lomond, the Arrochar Alps and the Cowal hills.

Distance: 15 _ miles
Grade: moderate/hard
Terrain: the route starts with a long slow ascent to the Harelaw roundabout. From here it mainly short inclines interspersed with long level sections. The road from Yieldshields to Kilncadzow is challenging for a time. However a long fast downhill follows directly. The final climb into Lanark is steep.
Map: OS Landranger sheet 72

BY THE WAY

YIELDSHIELDS
Yieldshields is a pleasant if unremarkable hamlet. The only reason to stop would be to picnic in the small public park.

KILNCADZOW (pronounced kilcaigie)
The remarkable bakery by the A721 serves up gargantuan homemade cakes, meringues and sausage rolls. At over 1000 feet above sea level the views from Kilncadzow can be superb.

CARTLAND
This tiny hamlet is a burgh of Barony and was granted its charterin 1607. The wooded knoll to north east may have been a lookout position built by Edward I as part of the defences around Lanark.

MOUSE VALLEY (pronounced moose)
An ancient native woodland fills the Mouse valley and is designated a national nature reserve. The woodland survives because it was difficult to harvest the wood from the steep sides of the Cartland crags, downstream, and the Cleghorn glen, upstream.

Jerviswood house, a 16th century tower house, overlooks the valley from high on the left. The house was the home of Robert Baillie, a Covenanter, who was executed in 1684 for allegedly being one of the plotters in the Rye House plot to assassinate King Charles II in 1683.

THE ROUTE

	Grid ref.	Miles
1.	886 436	0

Start: Lanark railway station. Leave the station car park and turn right. Go straight through at traffic lights and follow High Street downhill. Go through narrow gap at foot of High Street.

| 2. | 880 437 | 1/4 |

100 yards beyond narrow gap turn right, signed – A706, Linlithgow and Forth.
Follow A706 out of Lanark.

| 3. | 905 452 | 2 1/4 |

At traffic lights turn left over narrow bridge. Climb moderately to level crossing. Continue along road to roundabout.

| 4. | 917 472 | 3 1/2 |

At roundabout go straight ahead, signed – A706, Linlithgow and Forth.

| 5. | 918 474 | |

150 yards beyond roundabout turn right. Continue along road to T-junction at small collection of houses.

| 6. | 936 493 | 5 |

Turn left and continue to crossroads with A706.

| 7. | 923 506 | 6 1/4 |

Go straight over A706 onto Yieldshields Road. Follow road for 3 miles (continue past Springfield nursery and equestrian centre).

| 8. | 873 507 | 9 1/2 |

Once in the hamlet of Yieldshields take the first left onto Lymes Road. Fast descent followed by moderately steep climb to over 1000 feet. Short fast descent to A721.

| 9. | 884 487 | 10 3/4 |

Turn left and then right. Descend through Kilncadzow. Watch out for severe S bend.

| 10. | 883 467 | 12 |

Turn right over railway and follow road round to right to fork in the road. Take right fork and continue parallel to railway line. Follow road to Cartland.

| 11. | 866 462 | 13 1/4 |

In Cartland follow road round to the left and climb out of Carltland towards Greentowers farm. Road then descends gently at first but becomes very steep at houses.

| 12. | 876 455 | 14 |

Beyond bungalow follow the road round to the right – very fast twisting downhill takes you over the Mouse. Steep climb out of valley follows – poor visibility.

| 13. | 877 442 | 15 |

At top of hill turn left onto Wheatlandside and climb gently through housing Go straight over at crossroads and continue to T-junction.

| 14. | 882 443 | 15 1/4 |

Turn right and then turn right again.

| 15. | 881 440 | |

Beyond fire station turn left and then take second right past Tesco. At the foot of the hill turn left. Dismount at top of hill and push bike to High Street.

16.   **884 436**   **15 1/2**

Take right fork, Bannatyne Street. Follow to railway station.

17.   **886 436**   **15 1/2**

End: Lanark railway station.

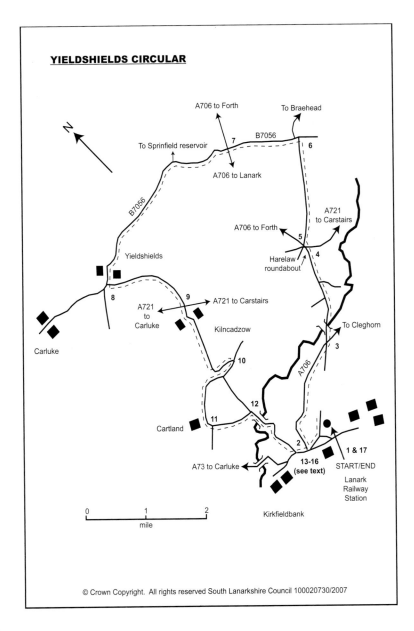

YIELDSHIELDS CIRCULAR

A706 to Forth

To Braehead

To Sprinfield reservoir

B7056

7

6

A706 to Lanark

B7056

A721 to Carstairs

A706 to Forth

5

4

Yieldshields

Harelaw roundabout

8

9

A721 to Carstairs

A721 to Carluke

Kilncadzow

To Cleghorn

Carluke

3

10

A706

12

11

Cartland

1 & 17

2

13-16 (see text)

START/END

A73 to Carluke

Lanark Railway Station

0   1   2
mile

Kirkfieldbank

KIRKFIELDBANK, HAWKSLAND AND GREENRIG

This is a short route that follows the quiet dyke-lined lanes linking the small farming communities of Hawksland, Dickland and Greenrig.

Sticking to the high ground between the valleys of the Nethan and the Clyde means very good views in all directions.

As it is a short ride you may wish to make the detour followed by a short walk to the Bonnington Linn – the furthest upstream of the falls of Clyde.

Distance: 8 miles
Grade: moderate
Terrain: the first hill out of Kirkfieldbank is challenging. Otherwise there isn't anything more than a short moderate incline and there are some good downhill sections to compensate.
Map: OS Landranger sheet 72

BY THE WAY

Once the first hill is out of the way it is a relatively easy cycle along narrow lanes with extensive views across a patchwork of fields marked out by mature broad leave trees – it is a classic rural scene. Tinto hill is particularly vivid and seems to loom around every bend.

From Greenrig there are very good views down the Clyde valley to Glasgow and beyond to Cowal, the Campsies and the Southern Highlands.

BONNINGTON LINN

A hundred yards beyond the turning for Lesmahagow (point 5) there is a left turn indicated as a dead end. This narrow road leads to a weir just upstream of the Bonnington Linn.

The Bonnington Linn is a complex and particularly inhospitable cataract. The river Clyde swings through 90 degrees to enter a gorge section which involves three further sets of falls.

Although this is not the biggest of the falls they can, when the river is in spate, be the most intimidating. Rocky pinnacles pierce the flow and the water is forced into narrow channels accentuating its power.

THE ROUTE

	Grid ref.	Miles
1.	863 438	0

Start: car park, village hall, Kirkfieldbank.

Turn right out of car park onto A72 and follow to next right.

2.	868 437	1/4

Turn right onto Riverside Rd. Follow uphill for 400 yards to fork in road a Whittinghame cottage.

3.	869 435	1/2

Take left fork. Follow uphill – steep in places. Follow round to right beyond Byretown farm to T-junction.

4.	873 416	2

Turn left and follow road for 1 1/4 mile.

5.	878 398	3 1/4

Take next right, signed – Lesmahagow.

Follow undulating road past Green Pastures to T-junction just beyond Birkhill farm.

6.	855 395	4

Turn right at T-junction. Follow road through farm to another T-junction.

7.	848 399	4 1/2

Turn right past row of houses built by John Frater. Continue for 100 yards to fork in road.

8.	850 403	4 3/4

Take left fork. Follow road downhill and round sharp right at Burnside. Climb past Greenhill farm.

9.	856 424	6 1/4

Road swings to the right at Greenrig. Good viewpoint. Fast descent into dip. Momentum enough to carry you out of dip to T-junction.

10.	865 427	6 3/4

Turn left and continue 100 yards to another T-junction.

11.	866 427	

Turn left and follow road round to the right at Newhouse farm and descend into Kirkfieldbank to T-junction with A72.

12.	868 437	7 3/4

Turn left and follow to village hall and car park.

13.	864 438	8

End: car park, village hall, Kirkfieldbank.

KIRKFIELDBANK,
HAWKSLAND
AND GREENRIG

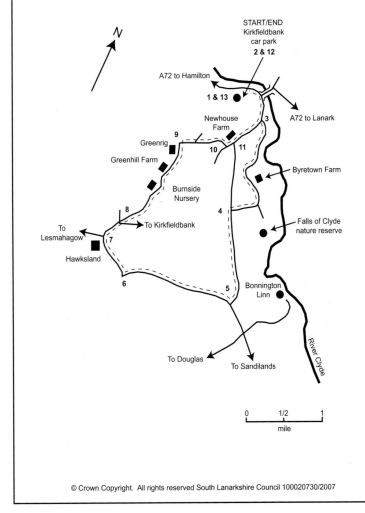

N

START/END
Kirkfieldbank
car park
2 & 12

A72 to Hamilton

1 & 13

3

A72 to Lanark

Newhouse
Farm

9

Greenrig

10

11

Greenhill Farm

Byretown Farm

Burnside
Nursery

4

8

To Kirkfieldbank

To
Lesmahagow

7

Falls of Clyde
nature reserve

Hawksland

6

5

Bonnington
Linn

River Clyde

To Douglas

To Sandilands

0   1/2   1
mile

THE STRATHAVEN ROUTES

The Common Green is at the heart of this attractive and bustling town well known for its own brands of ginger bread and toffee. High in amenities with some quaint touches it has long been a popular place to live for commuters working in Glasgow and music hall entertainer Sir Harry Lauder set up home here.

It was once the mills that provided the employment within the town and strenuous efforts were made to sustain the industry by responding to the trends of the day. Initially woollen mills they were adapted to weave linen then cotton and finally silk but to no avail.

In 1820 a group of Radical weavers marched from Strathaven under the leadership of James Wilson to Cathkin as part of a wider Radical rising to protest against the Corn Laws introduced in 1815. The Corn Laws forced up the price of wheat by blocking cheaper imports which inevitably had a knock on effect on the price of bread.

However the Strathaven Radicals dispersed, before reaching Glasgow, when they became aware that the reports of an armed rebellion and the imminent arrival of French troops were no more than rumours.

James Wilson was however arrested and tried as a traitor. He was hanged in Glasgow but his body was stolen and buried in Strathaven where he is revered as a hero. A monument to his memory was erected in 1846 – the year the Corn Laws were repealed.

Strathaven was also a centre for Covenanting activity during the 17th century. The Covenanter lords Montgomery, Loudon, Boyd and Lindsay seized Strathaven Castle in 1639 when hostilities with the Royalists broke out.

Later the earl of Linlithgow garrisoned troops in the castle with the purpose of stamping out the illegal prayers meetings held by Covenanters out on the moors. Covenanters John Barrie and William Paterson – both buried in the town's graveyard – were executed within the castle walls.

It was also at Strathaven Castle that Claverhouse, along with 150 dragoons, stayed the night before his disastrous encounter with the Covenanters at the battle of Drumclog (see Strathaven, Loudon Hill and battle of Drumclog route).

The ruined 14th century castle sits behind a curtain of trees to the west of the Common Green. Built by the powerful Douglasses it transferred to the Stewarts and finally to the Hamiltons.

There is also a rather macabre story associated with the castle. A wife of a lord of the castle displeased her husband so much that she was led to a purpose built niche. She was blessed by a priest, given some food and water and then bricked up in the niche. Recently when a portion of the castle walls collapsed human remains were revealed.

GETTING THERE
ROAD

From the south: leave the M74 at junction 8 and follow signs for Strathaven and Kilmarnock A71.

From the north: leave the M74 at junction 6 and follow the A723 through Hamilton.

RAIL

Nearest railway station is Haimyres in East Kilrbride – 11 miles; half hourly service to and from Glasgow central.

EATING AND DRINKING
Strathaven (01357 -)

Tudor House	4a Common Green	529487
Soaves	13 Barn St	521022
Taal	2 Bridge Street	522555
Tavern of the Town	16 Townhead Street	520184
Trattoria Da Mario	1 Wellbrae	522604
The Waterside	31 Waterside Street	522588
India India	10-12 Green St	522717
Rissons Restaurant	18 Lethame Road	520234

EATING AND DRINKING AND STAYING

The Strathaven Hotel	Hamilton Road	01357 521778

STAYING
Strathaven (01357 -)

The Shieling	Lesmahagow Road	520477
Springvale Hotel	18 Lethame Road	521131
Fred Taylor Millwell Farm	Chapleton	243248
D Simpson	The Steading, East Coldstream	522326

Blackwood, Kirkmuirhilland Lesmahagow (01555 -)

Dykecroft Farm	Kirkmuirhill and Lesmahagow	892226
Hopehill Cottage	22 Vere Road, Blackwood	893249
The Kerse B&B	The Kerse, Lesmahagow	894545

STRATHAVEN, SANDFORD AND LESMAHAGOW

This route follows the course of a Roman road across rolling farmland. Using mainly quiet back roads there are however short sections on the slightly busier B7086. On the return leg the character of the route changes. The route climbs out of the Nethan valley onto high lonely moors grazed by sheep.

Distance: 20 miles
Grade: moderate
Terrain: it is a fast downhill out of Strathaven but your momentum won't quite carry you to the top of the hill that follows. Beyond Sandford the route is either downhill or flat. The downhill into Lesmahagow is very satisfying but consequently the climb up to over 1000 feet starts almost immediately. There are however opportunities for you to get your breath back and once the high point has been attained the cycling is easy.
Map: OS Landranger sheet 72.

BY THE WAY

SANDFORD

Sandford is charming hamlet that has retained much of its original character. Nearby are the peculiarly named Spectacle E'e falls, so called because a young man took his revenge on his truelove's disapproving father by placing a pair of spectacles in the thatch of the father's mill.

A blaze resulted and the mill was razed. The new mill and the adjacent falls that powered it were from then on referred to as the Spectacle E'e. There is a short signposted walk to a viewing platform beneath the falls.

The road beyond Sandford becomes conspicuously straight as it takes up the course of a Roman road. At breaks in the high hedges and trees that line the road the views are very good. The next hamlet, Boghead, reeks of its mining heritage.

LESMAHAGOW

Lesmahagow has always had its mind on ecclesiastical matters. In 1144 Benedictine monks from Kelso established a priory on land granted by David I. The remains of the priory lie to the right of the imposing Old Parish Church.

The Lesmahagow Missal, specially written for the priory in 1240 was fortunate to survive the Reformation and is now in the National Library in Edinburgh.

The town was also a hotbed of Covenanting activity. At one point soldiers from the Highland Light Infantry were permanently stationed in the town to control the unrest.

Numerous covenanters, some of whom died in bizarre circumstances, are commemorated in the churchyard.

The Fountain, 9 Abbeygreen – 893237; Azzuri Bistro Italiano, 14 Abbeygreen – 895921; Pardesi Daba, 18 Abbeygreen – 890024; Jerry's Chinese Cuisine, 12 Priory Road – 890088; Star Inn, 515 Carlisle Road – 892293.

WATERSIDE

This is a particularly pleasant spot where trees shade an old sandstone bridge over the Logan Water. A sign points up hill towards Skellyhill farm to a monument to David Steel, a Covenanter who was captured and shot dead by Lieutenant Chricton of the Highland Light Infantry. Steel's namesake and descendent was the first presiding officer in the Scottish Parliament.

THE ROUTE

	Grid ref.	Miles
1.	702 445	0

Start: Strathaven Common Green.
Leave the Common Green on Bridge Street - off to the left from the top end of the green. Emerge at T-junction opposite the castle.

2. 704 445
Turn right and then left at the Castle Tavern. Follow Todshill Road to T-junction.

3. 704 443
Turn left onto Lesmahagow Road and continue past the fire station. Fast downhill out of Strathaven over the river Avon and then moderately uphill.

4. 718 429   1 1/4
At the top of the hill turn left at crossroads, signed – Sandford 1/4, Stonehouse 3. Cross the iron bridge and turn right in Sandford to climb past the village green to T-junction.

5. 719 430
Turn right at T-junction and leave Sandford on level road. Ignoring side roads follow this road for 3 miles to T-junction with B7086.

6. 761 420   4 1/2
Turn left onto B7086 and gently descend into Boghead.

7. 778 421   5 1/2
Turn right in Boghead onto Lesmahagow Road and follow out of Boghead. Fast descent all the way to T-junction in Lesmahagow.

8. 814 403   8
Turn right and continue into Lesmahgow.

9. 814 398
From Church Sq turn right onto Main Street and take first left at the community library – Bakers Brae.

10. 813 399
At the top of Bakers Brae turn left onto New Trows Rd. Climb steadily out of Lesmahagow.

11. 807 392   8 3/4
As gradient eases turn right, signed – Waterside 2, Strathaven 10. Climb on narrow red road past Birkwood Mains followed by a sharp left then right.

12.   803 386   9 1/4

When straight on is indicated as a dead end, turn left. Continue gently downhill past Middletown farm and Divity.

13.   790 371   11

Descent quickens to Waterside. Continue straight on, signed – Strathaven 8. (Skellyhill Covenanters Mon. is to the right). Road climbs to over 1000 feet at Brackenridge farm. Long decent to T-junction with B7086 at Deadwaters.

14.   751 417   14

Turn left onto B7086 and follow for one mile passing Yardbent and Castlebrocket.

15.   732 421   15

Take easy to miss left on bend. Follow road round to the left at Westhouse (old signpost points to Muirkirk). Cross straight over at Roman road and continue to T-junction with B743.

Spectacle E'e Falls

16.   687 422   18

Turn right downhill and cross bridge over river Avon.

17.   687 426   18 1/4

Take right immediately after crossing bridge and climb moderately into Strathaven on Newtown Road. Emerge at T-junction opposite fire station.

18.   704 442   20

Turn left and follow road to the right, signed – Kilmarnock, East Kilbride and Paisley. Follow Todshill Street past castle and Drumclog Arms. At T-juntion go straight over pushing bike over the pedestrian section to Common Green.

19.   702 445   20

End: Strathaven Common Green.

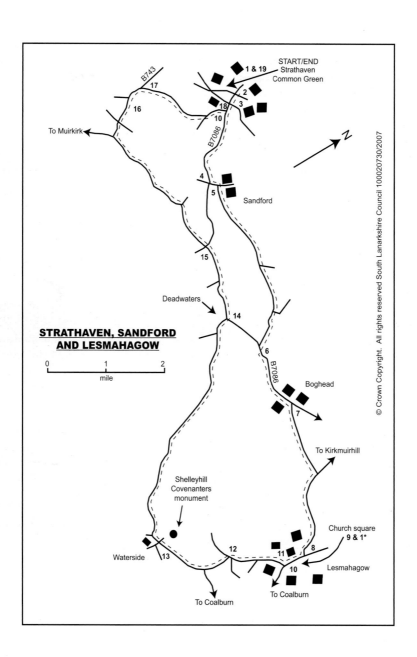

STRATHAVEN, SANDFORD
AND LESMAHAGOW

START/END
Strathaven
Common Green

1 & 19

B743

17

16

To Muirkirk

18

10

B7086

2

3

4

5

Sandford

15

Deadwaters

14

6

B7086

Boghead

7

To Kirkmuirhill

Shelleyhill
Covenanters
monument

Church square
9 & 1*

12

11

8

Waterside

13

10

Lesmahagow

To Coalburn

To Coalburn

N

0   1   2
        mile

STRATHAVEN, LOUDOUN HILL AND THE BATTLE OF DRUMCLOG

The quiet lane out of Strathaven, except for a short dash on the A71, sets the tone for the whole day. There are no villages or towns en route but the day is still entertaining. The gently undulating road bumps alongside the Avon Water, providing perfectly peaceful and carefree cycling.

Looping around the distinctive Ayrshire landmark of Loudoun Hill where Robert the Bruce won a famous battle you then encounter the site of the battle of Drumclog where the Covenanters won a rare victory against over government troops.

Distance: 17 1/2 miles
Grade: easy
Terrain: there are little more than gentle undulations to deal with. There is only one short climb at Loudoun Hill that is noticeably steep.
Map: OS Landranger sheet 71

BY THE WAY

DUNGAVEL

The controversial detention centre of allegedly illegal immigrants at Dungavel was once a home of duke of Hamilton. It is thought that Nazi Rudolf Hess was attempting to reach Dungavel when his plane crashed near Eaglesham.

LOUDOUN HILL

The craggy outline of Loudoun hill looms on your left. A volcanic plug its bluffs are very popular with rock climbers and although it doesn't appear so the walk to the summit it relatively straightforward if care is taken to avoid its rocky flanks. From the summit the views are extensive and it likely that Loudoun hill was an important lookout point, which could explain the proximity of two battle sites.

At the point where you leave the A71, Robert the Bruce won an important and morale boosting victory over the English troops under the command of Aymer de Valence. It was Bruce's second victory after his return to Scotland from his exile on Rathlin island.

THE BATTLE OF DRUMCLOG

Further on, at Mosside, limekilns can be seen embedded in the hillside opposite the low white cottage. Not far beyond Mosside a short detour takes you to the site of the battle of Drumclog where a large obelisk commemorates what was arguably the Covenanters' finest hour.

Short of the battlefield is a further memorial to the battle: a seminary (now a private home) built by the duke of Hamilton for the education of ministers. It is an indication of the importance attached to the events of June 1679.

John Graham of Claverhouse, also known as Bloody Calverhouse and Bonnie Dundee, was patrolling for illegal conventicles with 150 dragoons. The night before the battle they stayed at Strathaven Castle and aware of their presence the Covenanters were able to prepare for an encounter and deliberately selected soft ground on which to hold their conventicle, so as to thwart an attack by government horsemen.

Claverhouse did attack the coventicle and in the ensuing battle 30 dragoons were killed. Claverhouse was knocked from his horse but managed to skilfully mount his trumpeter's horse to make his getaway.

It was a huge fillip to the Covenanter cause and three weeks later 4 000 converged on the banks of the Clyde at Hamilton only to routed at the battle of Bothwell brig by the duke of Monmouth.

THE ROUTE

	Grid ref.	Miles
1.	702 445	0

Start: Common Green, Strathaven.
Leave the Common Green by Bridge Street, at the top left of the Green. Continue to the T-junction opposite the castle.

2. 704 445
Turn right and then left at the Castle tavern. Follow Todshill Road to T-junction.

3. 704 443
Turn left onto Lesmahagow Road.

4. 704 442 1/4
Take next right at fire station onto Newtown Road and follow out of Strathaven and on to T-junction with B743.

5. 687 426 1 1/2
Turn left and cross bridge over the Avon Water.

6. 687 423
Warning triangle alerts you to impending right turn. Make right turn (unsigned). Follow road ignoring all side roads.

7. 649 371 6
Road eventually descends to a unobvious junction with B745. Turn right, signed – Kilmarnock B745. Cross narrow bridge and then go straight on which effectively means leaving the B745 for a minor road.
Continue along road and over hump-backed sandstone bridge. Once round bend descend to T-junction.

8. 613 371 8 1/2
At T-junction turn left onto A71 and make 100 yard dash along A71 and turn right at entrance to sand and gravel works – battlesite.

9. 617 397 10 1/2
Take next left 1/2 mile beyond Mosside (straight on for battle of Drumclog).

10.   611 401   11

After 1/2 mile you arrive at a second T-junction at large white farm buildings – turn right. Follow very pleasant road across moorland planted with conifers and then by the Calder water. Follow to crossroads.

11.   647 433   14

At crossroads go straight over, signed Strathaven 4.

12.   684 442   16

At next junction turn left (if you find yourself on the A71 you've gone too far). After small rise turn right and descend into Strathaven through residential area to crossroads opposite Common Green.

13.   702 445   17 1/2

End: Common Green, Strathaven.

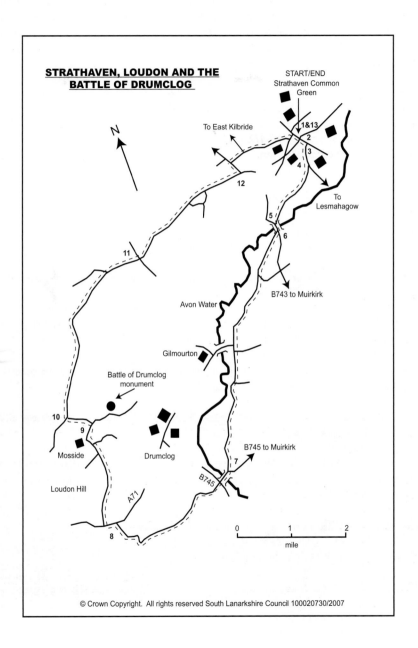

STRATHAVEN, LOUDON AND THE BATTLE OF DRUMCLOG

START/END
Strathaven Common Green

To East Kilbride

N

1&13

2

3

4

12

To Lesmahagow

5

6

B743 to Muirkirk

Avon Water

Gilmourton

Battle of Drumclog monument

11

10

9

Mosside

Drumclog

B745 to Muirkirk

7

Loudon Hill

B745

A71

8

0   1   2
mile

THE PACKMAN'S GRAVE (off-road)

This is a very straightforward and pleasant route ideal for as an introduction to off-road cycling. There is a very short section on the A71 but there is a wide grassy verge that can be used by less confident cyclists. The forestry section offers few views but once out the other side you it is worth stopping to take in the wild beauty of the youthful Avon as it passes through rocky gorges.

Distance: 10 miles
Grade: moderate
Terrain: all inclines are gentle and occasionally moderate. All off-road surfaces are good although the grassy track at the start of the off-road section can be soft.
Map: OS Explorer sheet 334

THE ROUTE

	Grid ref.	Miles
1.	639 399	0

Start: Drumclog parish church.
Follow B745 south away from A71 past trout fishery.

2.	646 368	1 1/4

At crossroads go straight on and follow level road past building emblazoned with Weavers Tavern.

3.	649 361	1 3/4

Go through gate beyond 'tavern' and after a short distance turn right uphill and follow switchbacks to join rough track and go to the left.

4.	647 349	2 1/2

Follow broad grassy track through field all the way to gate at entrance to forestry. Go through gate and follow forestry road. Road climbs steadily.

5.	620 343	4 1/2

At fork by small loch take the left fork. Track descends to cross the Avon Water and then climbs to another fork - keep to the right.

6.	605 360	6

Continue to Burnhead Farm. Route passes through farmyard and there is likely to be livestock or machinery in use – approach slowly and if necessary wait for the direction of the farm workers.

7.	600 368	6 1/2

Follow farm road from Burnhead to T-junction with minor road.

8.	608 371	7

Turn right and descend to junction with A71.

9.		

Turn right onto A71 and follow for 500 yards. You may wish to use the wide grassy verge. Take next right. Follow pleasant minor road all the way to crossroads. Turn left at crossroads to return to Drumclog.

10.	639 399	10

End: Drumclog parish church. (see map page 96)

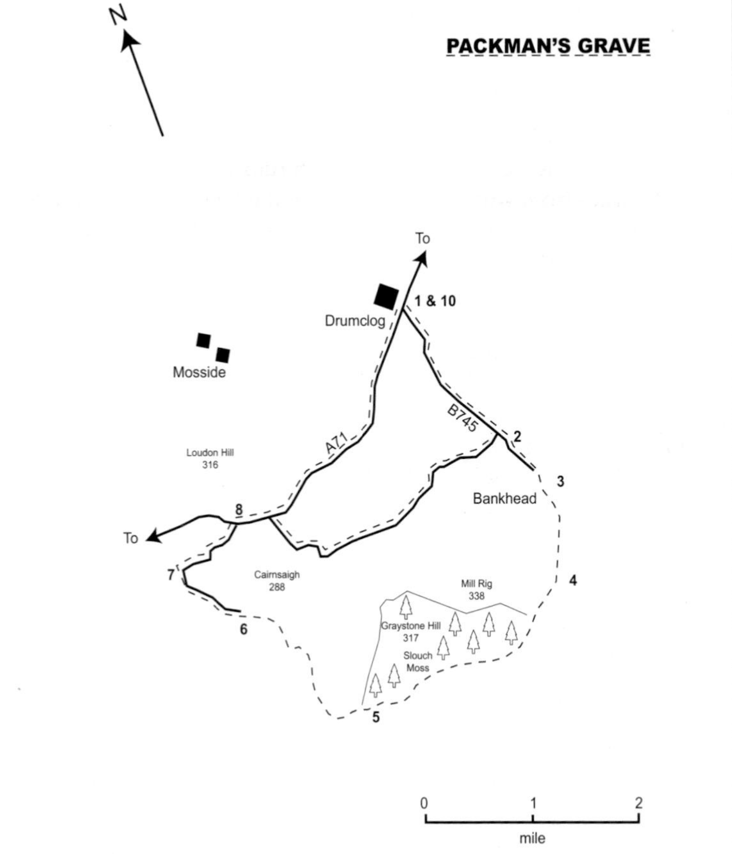

PACKMAN'S GRAVE

N

To

1 & 10

Drumclog

Mosside

A71

B745

2

Loudon Hill
316

3

8

Bankhead

To

7

Cairnsaigh
288

Mill Rig
338

4

Graystone Hill
317

Slouch
Moss

6

5

0	1	2

mile

OTHER ROUTES

CARRON VALLEY MOUNTAIN BIKING CENTRE
Volunteers have created 11 km of trails in a forest in the Carron Valley. All four trails are graded red. More information: www.carronvalley.org.uk

AIRDRIE TO BATHGATE
Part of the NCN 75, this traffic free railway path runs between Drumgelloch station in Airdrie and Bathgate from where you can follow the Union Canal and minor roads to the Falkirk wheel. The railway line between Airdrie and Bathgate is currently being re-instated which means the cycle route will be temporarily closed and eventually re-routed.
Up to date information:
www.sustransorg.uk; www.airdirebathgateraillink.co.uk

MORE NORTH LANARKSHIRE ROUTES
Cumbernauld to Glasgow; Airdrie to Longriggend; Castlecary to Longriggend; Shotts to Blackridge; Carluke to Shotts; Kirkintlloch to Campsie hills. Further details: www.northlan.gov.uk - click on sports facilities in menu and then cycling.

NCN 74
Otherwise known as Lochs and Glens (South). A large part of this route passes through Lanarkshire and is in long sections traffic free. Some of the routes in this book take advantage of it. It is also a good route for those cycling from Lands End to John O'Groats. Maps and leaflets available for download at: www.sustrans.org.uk

SCOTTISH BORDERS
The Tweed cycleway runs for 89 miles from Biggar to Berwick-upon-Tweed. However the route is signposted from the railway station at Carstairs Junction. The cycleway more or less follows the river Tweed taking in the Border towns of Peebles, Melrose, Kelso and Coldstream. More information at: www.visitscottishborders.com

DUMFRIES AND GALLOWAY
Details of KM (Kirkpatirck MacMillan) Trail, the National Byway and routes around Drumlanrig Castle at www.drumlanrig.com

USEFUL WEBSITES

www.outdoor-clydesdale.com

www.visitlanarkshire.com

www.visitscotland.com

www.spokes.org.uk

www.gobike.org.uk

www.visitscotland.com

TOURIST INFORMATION CENTRES

Abington, Welcome Break, Motorway Service Area,
Junction 13 M74, Abington, ML12 6RG – 01864 502436
Abington@visitscotland.com

Biggar, 155 High Street, Biggar, ML12 6DL – 01899 221066
Biggar@visitscotland.com

Lanark, Horsemarket, Ladyacre Road, Lanark, ML11 7LQ
Lanark@visitscotland.com

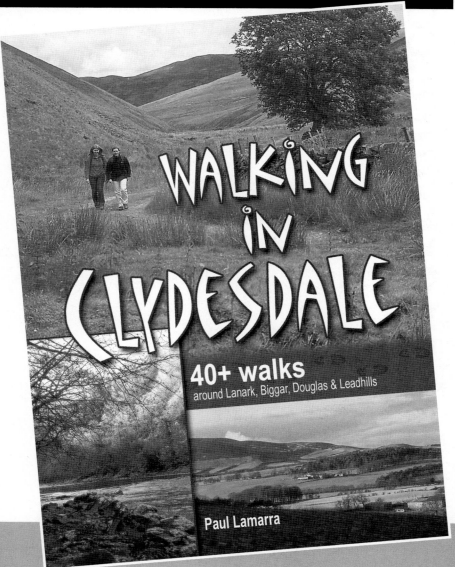

Visit Lanarkshire.com *Love it.*

Lanarkshire is a great place to visit with a wide range of attractions, activities and country parks which will appeal to all the family.

From the unique experience of New Lanark World Heritage site, Chatelherault Country Park and M&D's - Scotland's Theme Park, there really is something for everyone!

For more ideas on great days out in Lana

The area offers something for every visitor!

If you want to unwind, you'll enjoy the walking trails, country parks and cycle paths. If you seek adventure, try out some rock climbing, water sports or horse riding. If you crave some culture, be inspired by our museums, historic castles and industrial heritage.

By road or rail, Lanarkshire is less than an hour from Glasgow and Edinburgh!

e, log onto www.visitlanarkshire.com

Lanarkshire

NOTES

NOTES

NOTES

NOTES